they call it must be when completed a fine building - and
will I have no doubt prove a great
benefit to the Country - Lerwick is
under great obligations to Mr. Anderson
and that,

I was on reading!
ago. It take large
Dames generally g
we are as eager to have a pulling
Match with another boat, as boys

Miss Barbara Laing
Schoolhouse
Gulberwick

truly affect.
J. Jamieson

Some boats have taken as high as
scores or 40 cwt: of ling for one
trip. More she could not carry - Crops
rather aback -

Miss Laing

SHETLAND
A LOVE STORY

SHETLAND
A LOVE STORY

Kay Wheatcroft

M Sinclair

The Shetland Times Ltd.

Lerwick

2010

Shetland – A Love Story

ISBN 978 1 904746 47 8

First published by The Shetland Times Ltd., 2010.

Printed and published by
The Shetland Times Ltd.,
Gremista, Lerwick,
Shetland ZE1 0PX.

Shetland – A Love Story

An introduction

THE Shetland courtship of Robert Jamieson and Barbara Laing took place almost entirely by letter from 1858 to their marriage in 1861.

He was the schoolmaster at Sandness and she was the daughter of the schoolmaster at Gulberwick thirty miles away, too far to travel on a whim. Their 19th century lives were simple but hard, regulated by the landscape, the weather and the seasons, all of which are reflected in the beautiful 21st century photographs by Mark Sinclair.

Their touching letters tell the story of their lives, their work as teachers and farmers, his duties as postmaster and village scribe, their leisure and entertainment, local customs and events.

It is clearly their facility with words and their wry humour which attracted them to each other. As their correspondence continued, the seeds were sown for a strong and loving marriage.

ROBERT JAMIESON
1827-1899

BARBARA LAING
1838-1923

Whiteness 18ᵗʰ January 1858

My Dearest Barbara

It was my intention not to write you till after I had received the appointment to Sandness – but since I last saw you you have occupied so large a share of all my thoughts that I cannot delay any longer. For some time past I have not had a thought, a wish, that has not been of you and I now long to tell you that I sincerely, ardently and devotedly love you. I formed an attachment to you almost the first time I saw you, about two years ago, and ever since I have held you in the very highest estimation – you are so pleasing, so amiable, so modest and there is something in you so superior to other people that you insensibly gained my affections and I have not only esteemed, regarded, but adored you.

My love for you I have guarded with that jealous care with which misers guard their gold. I have kept it hidden in the recesses of my own soul. I considered it too sacred to be revealed to mortals – and the dread of your not returning it and my determination never to marry till I had a least the prospect of supporting a wife in some degree of comfort made me anxious to conceal it from you. For that reason I have avoided seeing you as much as possible because I knew well that if placed often in your company I would be unable to conceal my attachment and yet there have been times when I would have given all I possessed for a mere sight of you. Every time your name has been mentioned I have had to wage war with my feelings – have had to sustain a perfect struggle. I laboured under the impression that other people could not fail to detect what occupied my thoughts so entirely.

Without you I would feel as if life were a blank. Your every look and movement are engraven on my memory. I delight in associating you with every thing that is excellent – with every thing that is pure and lovely and I would not like to lose the idea of you for worlds.

Need I tell you how happy I shall feel if you will be kind enough to write me? Oh do it. I remember well what you said to me the morning on which I left you. I have often thought of it and have put two or three constructions on it. Did you mean that I was disagreeable to you? Or that you could not write me as you would like? If the latter I cannot accept it as an excuse – no fear of you – and you mistake me entirely if you think that I have any sympathy with wire-drawn scrawl and diction which instead of expressing feeling is intended to conceal it.

Do let me hear from you – it will give me so much pleasure. If you meant the former then I do not know what, but I will not anticipate. The mere thought of losing what I have for so long fondly cherished is painful. I know that you deserve a much better than I and how happy I could be if I had the power of rendering myself entirely worthy of you. But the most anxious solicitude to promote your happiness – the strongest, the purest affection and the most devoted attachment are all I can plead.

I am,

my dearest Barbara,

affectionately yours

Robert Jamieson

Gulberwick 27th January 1858

My dear sir,

I received your very kind letter on Friday but such a letter! I have often heard of 'love letters' and have seen a few which had the name, but till now I never had any idea what a real love letter was. Surely I am and always have been one of the happiest girls in the world! I have met with nothing but kindness from everybody all my life and now to be loved by such a man as you, how can I be but happy?

The reason why I told you that I could not write to you was that I did not like you to know how deficient I was both at writing and grammar. But if it is true that 'love is blind' perhaps you will never see my defects, so I will just try to do the best I can. You say that you did not intend to write me till after you had received the appointment to Sandness – I hope you did not think that would make me like you any better. If so you have been labouring under a mistake.

I love you, but it is neither as the schoolmaster of Sandness, or of Whiteness, but as Robert Jamieson. Yes, I love you for your own dear self and how can I help it? Nobody I think can know you properly and not love you in some way, you are so winning – and besides you are my father's best and truest friend. Indeed I was half in love with you before I became acquainted with you by hearing Father speak of you and by seeing your letters.

I am constantly thinking of you. I have tried every means in my power to banish you from my mind, at least for a time; but it's all of no use.

I can never make out how it was you came to love me. It is really wonderful! You are the most generous noble-hearted man I ever saw and I love you more than you can ever know. I would rather have a corner in your heart than be loved by all the fickle young fellows daily to be met with.

With kindest love,

your loving

Barbara L Laing

Whiteness 1st February 1858

My dearest love

Your charming little letter gave me the greatest pleasure imaginable and I have been in a state of hilarity ever since. The belief that you love me makes me happy and I care for nothing besides. How utterly trivial seem all the cares of life! In what beautiful colours does busy fancy paint the future and how she roams amidst scenes of purest happiness.

Mr James Johnston contracted on Saturday last. There was but a small company of us, but we enjoyed ourselves remarkably well. The night was showery and very stormy – so much so that when I was on the top of Wormadale hill it blew 'as if it had blown its last'. A very short time after I had, according to parliamentary phrase, taken my seat, tea was served. There were cakes, biscuits, loaves and I do not know what else. The bride behaved remarkably well. My opinion of her rose considerably. She spoke but little and was kind and courteous to all. She was dressed in a white figured muslin dress with two flounces – a very small blue silk napkin around her neck and fastened in front with a brooch, a cap ornamented with ribbons and flowers and gold coloured bracelets on each arm. She really looked very well. He wore a black shooting coat, brown trowsers, a grey vest and neck tie. I do not believe that such a night of fun and glee was ever seen in Linkster before. I have been invited to the wedding about twenty times. I shall behave like a real good boy, shall observe every thing and tell you all.

9th February: My friend's wedding was celebrated with all the pomp and splendour of rural festivity. When I arrived I found the house, which is rather a small one, densely crowded and the parish minister and his daughter seated one at each side of the fire. The company was arranged in four lines so closely that there was scarcely room to move. In the third line right opposite the fire the bride and bridegroom were seated. On her left was the best maid, the bridegroom's sister, and on his right was the best man, the laird of G-. The bride was dressed in a white muslin dress with three flounces. Her cap was fringed and overlaid with a glittering silver coloured lace and at each side were a rose and a flower resembling a snowdrop. I hate and detest and abhor these caps and believe that brides would look much prettier if they would throw them to the dogs and be married in their bare heads.

The ceremony commenced. All arose as if by instinct and when these thrilling words were pronounced "I declare you married persons" the bride's bosom heaved convulsively. Poor thing! A new era in her existence that moment commenced. A glass of wine was offered to each and the bride's cake was freely distributed. I looked attentively for the ring but believe that some one had swallowed it as I heard of none who found it.

I never attended a better wedding. Supper was announced at 10.30 and about two hours after we set out for the future residence of the newly married couple. When we came in sight of the house a perfect flood of light burst upon our view. It was brilliantly illuminated – a number of candles being placed in each window and at a distance the appearance was beautiful. We saw them into the nuptial chamber and then bade them Adieu. I have visited them twice since and they are living like two doves.

I have thus, my dearest, given you a description of the wedding according to promise. When I see you I shall tell you any thing I may have omitted.

With fondest love, your own devoted

Robert Jamieson

Gulberwick 26th February 1858

Dearest – well I'm sure I don't know what to call you. Mr Novelist? Jamieson is too long, Robert does not come natural to me somehow, and besides it is a very matter-of-fact name. Bobby is too childish, it would not suit you at all and Robin, well Robin sounds very well in poetry and I think it will suit you best. I will call you by that name this time and if you do not like it you can tell me and I shall not do it again.

Well, dear Robin, I am much obliged for your very particular account of Mr Johnston's contract and very nice description of the wedding. Poor Johnston! What will he do when you go to Sandness? I liked your last epistle to Father remarkably well. It made him laugh some and that was a great comfort. The story was very interesting and beautifully told. I don't believe you gave it in the man's own words. Common sailors cannot talk so well.

I was very happy while you were here. Happy to have you so near me and besides your presence sheds such a cheerful influence all around. Everybody seems happy and this is so pleasant. Oh how dull, how very dull it was after you went. Nobody seemed to know what to do and little Bobby kept saying in such a mournful voice "Jamieson's awa at Whiteness". I read, sung, sewed and attended to my duties all with the greatest assiduity in order to drive away time, but it seemed as if it never went so slowly.

Maria has been singing "Robin is my only Jo" and I have learned "The hazel dell", "Nelly Bly", "My dog Fray", "The village maiden", "Willie we have missed you", "Scots wha hae wi Wallace bled" and "Mary in Heaven" all to sing for you when you come here again. I send you a copy of another pretty little song which I have learned and you must give your opinion of it.

"Is there a sweet below
So sweet as love?
No joy doth mortals know
So sweet as love
Love cheers dear friends who part
Love doth its charms impart
To soothe the aching heart
How sweet is love!"

Now goodbye for the present and with kindest love,

I am your ever loving

Barbara L Laing

Happyhansel, Walls, 28th February 1858

Good evening, lovely

I am delighted to see you. The people have gone to the chapel in crowds and I am all alone. So, come, sit down here, and tell me how you are and how all my good friends in Gulberwick are. I hope Mr Laing will have a little volume of poetry to show me. If he continue at this rate he will ruin Rannie who was styled the "poet laureate of Zetland". Draw the chair nearer the fire.

I arrived here late on Friday night last. As I approached the house the barking of a dog inside was fierce and terrible. He must have mistaken me for a thief and a robber. Mr and Mrs Rannie were in bed and the poor old man was compelled to rise and open the door. He allowed me to see nothing but his head and after asking me if I was myself, fled back with the rapidity of a hare. I had scarcely entered the house when I heard the hearty ringing laugh of Mrs Rannie and in less than no time she was dressed and in the room. Had I been her son she could not have been more delighted.

I am sure you would be delighted with Walls. I consider it the most important parish in the island. The population in 1851 was 1224. There are eight merchants, four ministers, four kirks and I do not know how many fine looking houses in it. It is of considerable extent, uneven, rugged. It is principally green and there are houses in every direction – some in valleys and others as if anxious to breathe a purer air are placed on higher ground. Downawalls where the kirks and shops are looks more like a village than a country parish and Vaila, a long green isle opposite, the seat of the Scotts of Melby, and Vaila Sound improve the appearance remarkably.

Happyhansel is built on an eminence and the view is excellent, including the Weisdale and Delting hills. The house consists of four rooms with I do not know how many closets. The parlour is a comfortable room and the one in which I am writing is large and airy – a few shillings tastefully expended would make it a beauty. It is unquestionably the best school house in the island. The school room is on the end, was built in 1849 and is a good one.

You are not thinking to leave already? Wait a while longer. You must – it is on a heavy shower and you cannot go out till it be dry. Wait two minutes longer – one minute then – well, you won't stay. Good night to you then. Give my kindest love to Mr and Mrs Laing and the bairns and hope that you will always think kindly of your

ever loving

Robert Jamieson

c-o-m-e, a-g-a-i-n, a-s, s-o-o-n, a-s, y-o-u, c-a-n. O she is out of sight now.

Solus: well, that is the lovliest girl that ever was formed. She is so amiable and pleasing and I never saw nor read of any person like her except Milton's Eve on the first day of her creation. How I love her – I wonder if every person loves as I do. If they do how does it happen that there are so many unhappy marriages. Two or three times after I had posted her letters I felt a kind of terror – for fear that I might have said something which might not please her. I would rather displease the whole world. She is the lovliest of the lovely.

Gulberwick 12th June 1858

Cruel inconsiderate Robert!

If I only had you here I would give you a scolding that would dumbfounder you entirely. Can it be possible that you have ta'en the pet in consequence of my not writing? Surely you ought to have known better! Placed as I have been in a situation of such responsibility as that of nurse and housekeeper, how could you be so unreasonable as to expect that I could write? I know you must have been very disappointed on your return to Whiteness not to find a letter from me waiting for you, but you would have found two from Father. From the latest of these you would have learned what had occurred and if you had had any consideration, you would have understood the reason why there was none from me. But from your silence it would appear that you did not understand and that you have attributed it to every cause but the right one.

The very day on which I had intended to answer your letter my little brother was born and ever since then my time has been wholly occupied in attending to mother, the baby and the household affairs and you ought to have known that it was so. Indeed you need not have been surprised if I had even forgotten you entirely for a time, but it was not so. I did not, I could not forget you. I wish I could have done it, for then I would not have had the vexation of knowing how pettish and inconsiderate you are, for to what other cause can I attribute your silence?

Father has written three letters to you, to none of which he has received any answer as yet. You have not even congratulated him on the birth of his son. But for the newspapers which you returned we would not have known whether you were alive or not. When the newspapers arrived we overhauled them carefully, thinking that there might have been a letter in the folds but to our great disappointment we found nothing.

But after all, dear Robert, I may have been too severe on you. Perhaps you have been so much troubled about getting your things removed and getting settled at Sandness that it has been impossible for you to write; or worst of all you may be ill. If so I wish I were beside you, for I am such a capital nurse I would have you well in less than no time.

The birth of my little brother has interfered with all my arrangements. I had intended to read the "Education Course", to study French and practise writing and many other things during the summer, but now that is out of the question. Mother is so weak that it will be long before she is able to do anything and until she gets stronger I must be Guidwife. Father is speaking of giving up taking the "Family Paper". Now this is very provoking for it is becoming more useful and interesting than ever. In the last monthly part was the commencement of lessons in French, pronounciation and all. The first half yearly volume is now complete. Father must either give it up now or not till the end of another half year and we would have to break off in the middle of a very interesting tale by J. F. Smith.

Now I suppose you will be complaining that this is a very cold letter but I cannot always be talking of love like you, especially when I am in a hurry. This is a very poor affair every way but if you knew how stiff my hands are and what a flutter I am in you would excuse me.

Please write immediately if you have not already written for I am dying to hear from you.

Your affectionate

Barbara L. Laing

Sandness 16th June 1858

Come, come, dearest, be a loving, lovely girl as you are and let those scold who know no better. Look up, laugh a good laugh. Now, that's much better. Nothing like a good hearty round of laughter when one is out of humour. It clears the social atmosphere and is an excellent remedy for all the ills which humanity is heir to.

I excused your not writing but notwithstanding the multiplicity of your duties, I would really have been surprised had you forgotten me. I do not believe in the expression 'forget'. I believe that some where in the good old book the words 'She *may* forget' are to be found – I wish you would rise up and look in the book of Nehemiah or in the first chapter of Genesis and see if you could find it, but there is a pretty considerable difference between 'may forget' and 'forgotten entirely'.

I did not reach here till the 4th inst. And when I found myself settled I could not help giving a sigh of relief and wishing – guess what I wished for – I may as well tell it at once. I wished for you. The room I presently occupy is such a beautiful little thing, papered, oil painted, marble mantlepiece, fine brass grate, and I found every thing so neatly and tastefully arranged when I arrived that I wished for you heartily. I just thought how happy and pleased you would look.

I am not going to tell you how I love you, nor how much long I have thought for you till you promise never to call people 'cruel' or 'pettish' or 'inconsiderate' unless you are persuaded they are so. But I may tell you that I am often at Gulberwick – that altho' the breadth of the country lies between us, imagination sets distance at defiance and I hover around you continually – do you ever see me? And I often bring you here and such delightful times we have. I have taken you a dozen of times thro' the parish, have told you all I know about every spot we visited and have pointed out every place which I thought possessed the smallest interest.

I live retired, I associate with none, and therefore have no person to whom I can tell what I think and feel but yourself. There is a beautiful park adjoining the house thro' which I wander in the evenings. You are always with me and we have happy times. I have thought no long for Whiteness – I am ten – fifty times more comfortable here and have at least the prospect of doing much better.

I have been buried in Hugh Miller's "Schools and Schoolmasters" since Friday. It is grand. I hope you will not forget your French.

I have no objections to taking Cassells paper. The difficulty will be how to send it to you. What were the ideas you had formed of JF Smith? Does he not have a powerful beard? You would see that the story of his being a native of Lerwick is nonsense. There is an excellent tale going on in the meantime in Chambers Journal.

Remember me fondly to Maria. Tell me how you like your little brother and tell me all your news.

Your ever loving Robert Jamieson

Melby 23rd June 1858

My Lovliest Dear

I am delighted with Sandness – I never saw a prettier place. You will observe from the name that it is a ness and that there is abundance of sand in it. A dyke which runs along the foot of a ridge of hills encloses it on the South and on the West, North and East it is bounded by the rushing, rolling, roaring surges of the broad Atlantic, the turbulent sound of Papa Stour and the spacious Bay of St Magnus.

There are three churches in it, ministers visit it regularly, especially in summer and harvest and the people tho' rather outspoken and rough are very kind and obliging, much more so than the people of Whiteness are. Education is not in a very advanced state among them, but this is not to be wondered at. My predecessor's educational qualifications are very limited. His great strength lies in telling tales, which for wildness and improbability exceed anything in the "Arabian Nights" and to these his pupils would listen for hours with gaping wonder.

His best half has altered her tactics towards me. She now calls me her dear – but there is not the smallest need of your being the least jealous as she is getting on the other side of seventy and even in her best days has not been a very loveable article. She has lately received a large massive pair of gold earrings from her friends in Australia and is anxious to have her ears bored. Could you supply me with a stout rusty needle? She seems much attached to the soil, a part of the croft which is of excellent quality and yields good crops. She wishes she could take it with her but whether it be across the sound to a house they have taken in Papa or across the Jordan, I cannot say.

My pupil Jamie Peterson, poor fellow, is disconsolate. He had not been at school for three days and on Wednesday evening I was wondering what had become of him when he sent me the following laconic epistle: "I have just come from her I love – my prospects are miserable. The last ray of hope is nearly extinguished."

I wish you were acquainted with this fair one of his, that you could plead his cause. The thoughts of her for the last twelve months at least have nerved him to exertion and he has made astonishing progress in education. He has been here today and I find that he is tormented with doubts and fears and jealousy. The truth is he has never asked her yet. Let me tell you more. He would be glad if I would lend him my hand tomorrow night as he wants to give her something like a decent letter – and I have promised him all the assistance in my power.

With all the love in the world,

Your ever loving Robert Jamieson

Gulberwick 6th August 1858

My dear dear Robert

I had nearly given up hopes of ever hearing from you more when your letter arrived. When it was put into my hand it felt so little that I almost trembled for fear that it was merely a hasty retort to my peevish epistle but on opening it I was glad to find that it was only the thinness of the paper that made it appear so small.

I think you must have misunderstood what I said with regard to the "Family Paper". I did not mean that you should take it out in parts – I meant that you should wait till December when the next half yearly volume will be complete and then purchase it bound. But there will be no need of that now as Father is so well pleased with the French lessons that he is still going to take it.

There is going to be a wedding here next week. Do you remember taking notice of a girl in our Sunday school and remarking what an open agreeable countenance she had? Well she is the bride and the bridegroom is the lad who came here on Christmas eve with the skin for the cover of John and Thomas's football.

Father and Maria are from home and I have been left in charge of the school, a post which I really do not like and which I have had long enough this season to convince me that I was never intended for a schoolmistress, but I have learned to look angry and scold like anything. If you were only within my reach you should catch it – as a friend of mine used to say.

You seem to be delighted with Sandness, but you need not try to persuade me that it is prettier than Gulberwick. Oh, I wish you could see Gulberwick now. It is very beautiful and it will be still more so in a week or two. I believe you will not be able to see it now but you must not forget your promise to be here at my birthday.

Poor fellow Peterson. I am very sorry for him, but I hope that with your assistance he has now come to a right understanding with his sweetheart. I think he should have spoken to her sooner – made sure of her before any other came in his way. You must tell me how he has succeeded for I take a great interest in love affairs.

My little brother Arthur is a pretty little thing and I love him dearly. It is now two o'clock in the morning and what with bad pens and bad eyes I have made bad work of it, so must conclude

with kindest love, your loving

Barbara L Laing

Sandness 25th August 1858

My lovliest dear

I am truly glad to hear that you have been discharging the onerous duties of schoolmistress with so much efficiency and zeal and that you like them so very well.

How I wish I were a little boy at Gulberwick, with what glee I should enroll myself as one of your pupils and what beautiful funs I should have. I should laugh and whistle, blot my copy, tear my book and punch the boy nearest to me till he roared like a wild buffalo and then deny that ever I touched him. I should make amazing mistakes in my lessons, spell the words backwards, throw over the forms, speak at the top of my voice, make faces on the girls and when I had provoked you so much that you were obliged to call me up, instead of holding out my hand to receive the weight of the dreaded tawse I should throw my arm around your neck and k-k-k-k-kiss you (I always stammer very much in pronouncing that word – it surely is because I have no fancy for k-k-k-kissing) till I was tired – and afterwards be a good boy for the rest of the day. What would I not give to be a little boy at Gulberwick.

I am often hard pressed for a person to take charge of one of my classes. What do you think of engaging as one of my assistants? Never did mortal love an assistant so much as I should love you. We should work and read and study together. I have a severe attack of stammering tonight.

A letter came by the post today addressed to Jamie in something like a female hand. I hope it will be a messenger of peace, but he has not come for it yet.

I wish I could draw away time with my breath and thereby hasten the hour when I may see you again. You shed a cheering influence over me, just as the star beams lit up and cheer the path of the belated travellers, I take as much pleasure in thinking of you as the philosopher does in prosecuting the distances and magnitudes of the celestial bodies – and as each star is the centre of a system so you are the centre of my every earthly hope and pleasure, and as each planet in that system revolves round the centre so does my every thought and aspiration revolve around you.

I really would be glad to know if I have been able to convey to you anything like a correct idea of the depth, the strength, the intensity of the love I have for you.

With every blessing and 100 k-k-k-kisses,

I am your ever loving

Robert Jamieson

Melby 7th October 1858

My dearest,

Your birth day was a violent one. I had scarcely finished your letter when the rains began to descend and the winds to blow and to blow with a force and a fury quite remarkable – surely Boreas must have been in a very excited mood – in a towering passion. No person here – even that very respected individual the oldest inhabitant ever remembers the like. It cracked and bellowed on the roof like thunder – shutters flapped, doors rattled. It roared and shrieked through every hole and crevice, sometimes hoarse and fiercely, sometimes with a shrill peculiar whistle similar to a tuned instrument and sometimes with a dull moaning sound as if conscious that its violence however terrific could not last.

It rained and such rain. It rushed, it fell in torrents, it came streaming from roofs, it came rushing through walls, it came oozing through windows, it came lashing through doors. The foundations of some houses appeared broken up and tubs, buckets and pails were impressed into the service of baling. Lochs were swollen to three times their original size, meadows and cornfields were immersed some feet in water.

The sea – but who shall describe it? The pen of a Walter Scott would not be able to do it justice. I can give you no idea of it – it was one broad expanse of foam. On the night preceding the storm I never did see any thing so truly grand. The breakers were rolling mountains high and chasing each other to the shore – dashing themselves into foam which ascended in a cloud of mist into the air, receding and returning as if to the contest with renewed if not increased violence. The noise was terrible.

I could not sleep. About two o'clock in the morning I was out. It was awful and sometimes made me shiver. There was scarcely any wind, a few small black clouds floated through the atmosphere. Lightning was flashing vividly and the noise was so continuous, so tremendous, so everywhere that I could not tell whether it was in the sea, on the earth or in the air.

Don't mention this – but I tell thee lovely that we are a very advanced people. Mrs Pole told me last night that she knew in the first of the week that it was going to be a storm because the comet had such a long tail – she had remarked it.

With fondest love,

your ever loving

Robert Jamieson

Gulberwick 19ᵗʰ October 1858

My dear Robert

My time is so little at present that I doubt if I can write any thing worth reading and then the good old rule came into my mind,

> "Deal with another as you'd have
> Another deal with you
> And what you would not take again,
> Be sure you never do."

I am happy to inform you that the Queen of the Isles is safe and all her crew. Certainly my twentieth birthnight was a night to be remembered. What a grand description that was you gave! Poor me! I slept too sound to pay much attention either to the wind or the sea.

I am happy to hear you are so enlightened West yonder. We'll surely have good weather now, for both the Comet and its tail have quite disappeared. Was it not a beautiful sight?

I have had a good deal to take up my attention lately. There is a very nice little girl from town with us just now. She is rather delicate and needs a good deal of attention and as Mother has a baby of her own I thought it was my duty to attend to Leebie and I have found it a very pleasant duty. She had a baby sister who died, her mother was very ill and her father mad with drink (oh how I detest that man).

She is only ten years old and yet she is very far on with her education. She is very fond of reading and has a number of very nice little books, several of which she has got at school as rewards for diligence and good conduct. I have read some of them and I fear it was rather selfish for some of the time that was taken up in reading them might have been employed in writing to you, but if once I get hold of a book it is the hardest thing in the world for me to leave it until I have finished it.

I was very glad to hear there was a letter for Jamie. Whether it was a messenger of peace or a refusal it is better than to remain in suspense, but I hope it was the former.

I had a strange dream some nights since. I thought that I was in the garden and that I saw you on the road above Micklegarth as plainly as if you were only a few yards distant, going in the direction of Lerwick, riding on a little brown horse with both your crutches slung on its north side and I wondered why you were going to town. I concluded that you had some urgent business and that as soon as it was settled you would come and I felt very happy in the prospect of seeing you so soon, but I awoke and Oh how provoking! But away with dreams, I sincerely hope that I shall really see you soon.

So goodnight and with kindest love,

I am, dearest Robert, ever affectionately yours,

Barbara L Laing

PS please write again very soon.

Melby 5th January 1859

My dearest love

Another year with all its hopes, its joys, its griefs, its sorrows has now revolved into the great ocean of the Past. It is not only instructive but highly interesting to note the various viscisitudes which occur in that brief period of human existence called a year.

You were perfectly right in desiring me not to mention either teetotallers or teetotalism to your father any more and I was not intending to do it. I see he is very sore on that subject and am vexed that I should have given him the least cause.

It was very very imprudent in me to purchase the whisky, but I did it on the impulse of the moment and I had no more intention of offending him than I had of offending you. I saw that night that he was not pleased and think I mentioned it to you, but so far as I remember I ceased immediately after to take any notice of it and it was not till the morning I left that I learned that he was really offended and not a little surprised. The shyness in his manner I attributed to illness. The most awkward feature in the case is that he believes I did it with a design and no amount of explanation can remove this impression.

Except on certain occasions dram drinking is a custom not practised here. We are about 8 miles from the nearest public house, but our little dispute has made me a confirmed teetotaller. I hate even to think about it. I never had any particular fancy for it and therefore the want of it is no annoyance. When I was at Whiteness I used to feel disagreeable when a friend or a stranger called and I *had naething* to offer him. Visitors do not come often my way here, but when they do come the idea of apologising for the non appearance of a dram never strikes me. It is an expensive as well as a thankless kindness and when once begun must be continued.

Christmas day passed very quietly. I enjoyed my own reflections in the genuine bachelor style. The greater part of the day I spent in perusing the November numbers of the "John o Groat" which the postman had brought me from Walls and in which were no less than three letters on the Lerwick Kirksession case and one from Dr Robertson of Scalloway written in his original peculiar style in reply to a traveller who had, sometime in the month of July last, eaten the flesh of a pig in the doctor's house which tasted so strongly of fish that it could have been fed with nothing but "the refuse of a fishing station". The doctor says that had the traveller "been a *gryce* and lived with Louis the 18th in the Tuileries he could not have been better fed". The traveller must have been a particular shabby one.

I had a letter from my pupil Jamie Peterson last week. He has, he says, banished all thoughts of his hard hearted fair one and does not intend to send her even a newspaper.

I shall be longing and expecting as much as ever to hear from you again. With kindest kindest love and and and a thousand kisses,

Your ever loving

Robert Jamieson

Gulberwick 26th February 1859

My dear Jamieson

It is now near the time when the great snow was the last year and I have been thinking a great deal about the pleasant times we had then and wishing that we could have had such a time again. O was it not a happy time? I love to think of it. Maria says that she wishes she had the power to bring a snow like the last year's and to bring you along with it and then we should have a time of it.

I have not told you that my cousin Arthur made me a beautiful Christmas present in the shape of the complete poetical works of the great American poet Longfellow. It is handsomely done up in cloth with gilt edge and eight steel engravings. Was it not very kind of him?

I was very glad to hear that your school gave so much satisfaction. I rather think Mr Nicoll admired it though you were too modest to say so. You must have had a very laborious time of it this winter, having to keep school both day and night. I hope it has not injured your health. I have been thinking now for a day or two that you are perhaps unwell. I cannot get rid of the thought and shall feel uneasy till I hear from you.

I had intended to have written much more but time will not permit me at present, so good bye dearest,

your loving

Barbara L Laing

Melby 3rd March 1859

My dearest love

I shall respond first to the concluding sentence of your last letter. I am quite well and have been so not only since you heard from me last, but ever since I saw you last. I have however for some weeks felt very dull. There is scarcely a man left in the parish – and what is even more singular it is a rare sight to see a man child – all are off for Greenland.

My pupils are reduced to the number twelve, my nearest neighbour whose door is about twenty paces from mine and who visited me often during the winter evenings – and what with his tales of what he had seen and with mine of what I had not seen we managed to pass the time pleasantly enough – goes south per steamer on Monday first and rests not till he finds himself in the auriferous fields of Australia. Captain Sinclair, my other neighbour, has taken it in his head to build a house at Whiteness and is from home also and, except for very brief periods, will not I am afraid be much more at Sandness.

I have just finished "Kenilworth" by Sir Walter Scott, one of the most intensely interesting of all the works of that celebrated author which I have read. I was glad to hear that your cousin had presented you with a copy of H.W. Longfellow's poems. What do you think of Evangeline? And does your copy have "Hiawatha"? This winter Hugh Miller has been my favourite author. His works are here and I have perused them all with thorough admiration.

Now good night to you lovely and just give me one kiss before we part – another one – one yet – one more – you are my dearest love – a sound sleep to you – and I hope that you will dream of your ever loving

Robert Jamieson

Gulberwick 7th March 1859

My dear Jamieson

I have been reading "Ruth Hall" by Fanny Fern lately and I never read any thing I like better. I do love Fanny's way of writing. She speaks straight to the heart. Whatever side she takes, she is sure to carry the sympathies of her readers along with her. Nobody I'm sure – unless they be like Ruth's cousin, Mr Millet alias 'the wooden man', can read "Fern Leaves" or "Ruth Hall" through and through without having to drop the book now and then in consequence of something like a mist coming over their eyes. If you have not seen Ruth Hall you must get it and read it. I'm sure you will be delighted with it. Father and Mother both say it is the most natural thing they ever read.

"Hope Evermore" ended beautifully. Hope went through great trials, poor thing. But it all came right at last.

Now dearest, I must bid you good bye for it is nearly three o'clock in the morning, I am dearest Jamieson,

your affectionate Barbara

Melby 28th March 1859

I am sorry, truly sorry, my darling love, that I fear it will be entirely out of my powers to see you this spring. A chat would now be a luxury and as for a kiss gosh! It would be a felicity. I wish I had wings – I should to night use them and should take you by surprise.

Delivering has commenced here in real earnest. I began last week and am progressing as yet favourably. Today I have nine persons labouring away as fast as they can. I was unable to procure more than two servants as here, owing to the men all leaving for Greenland, they are very scarce indeed, so that I must employ people by the day and I don't like to go away and leave them. When I will have finished is what I cannot say. Under even favourable circumstances I do not think it will be earlier than the 20th May.

Hughie who was with me during the winter is now away at Greenland and the *chiel* I have in his place is a curiosity. He is a native of Aithsting, but has lived in this parish for some years. He is nineteen years of age, can read none and his organ of numbers is utterly entirely deficient – he can literally count none. His friends are few indeed and as he was quite unmanageable few will keep him. The last house he was in they belaboured him soundly, but they might as well have thrashed at a peat stack. I engaged this boy whom nobody thought worth the keeping and he has laboured since he came to the house with a zeal and an earnestness and an amount of physical power which half surprises me. For instance in four days he collected, quarried and laid on the spot as many stones as will build thirty fathoms of a dyke.

Have you ever tried French since? I began to it anew some weeks ago but the delving has hurled every thing out of my head. What did you think of Isa Craig's poem on Burns?

I hope that you will not be the least offended at my not coming to Gulberwick. I would be most happy to come if I could.

With kindest love, your ever loving

Robert Jamieson

Melby 6th May 1859

My dearest Love

I spent this week twelve months ago with you and memory which is ever busy recalls and hovers over every incident and every moment of that very pleasant time.

I remember the dreadful day of rain and storm which prevented my leaving home as I intended and the annoyance which it caused me – my walk across Wormadale hill on the following morning. I remember my admiration of the beautiful situation of Scalloway and its surrounding scenery as viewed from the summit of the hill to the Eastward, and the thoughts which must occur to everyone on beholding its ruined and decayed castle within whose walls scenes of festive mirth, of disorder and of violence have been enacted.

I remember my leisurely walk along the Scalloway road from which the view is as dull as bleak, as dreary as can well be witnessed anywhere, my emotion on seeing Gulberwick, quiet and still with its fields but newly cultivated, its bay unmoved by the gentlest ripple and the ocean stretching away in the distance as far as the eye could reach, calm, smooth and glassy – an emblem of tremendous power in repose.

I remember my gladness at seeing you and the sort of revulsion of feeling on observing your shyness which bore such a strong resemblance to dislike and which caused me to spend a night of torture, not the less real because it was imaginary, the explanations and the happy, thrice happy hours we afterwards spent. I should like to live them over again. Should like to reckon them twice as the luminous spots in my existence to which I can in after years revert with pleasure.

I should like to see you, to pet you, to tell you how I love you. I regret that such a distance intervenes between us but it cannot be helped. To have seen you this week would have given me much pleasure. I am longing to see you much, but could not come. At the same time this is not the very best season for visiting, every person is so busy and "balmy sleep weary nature's kind restorer" is apt to visit us with the approach of "the shades of night".

Summer has it seems set in already. Ever did you see such beautiful weather? The very *maws* are enjoying it. My oats and potatoes were finished on Friday. I don't know how much oats I have sown, but I have planted about seventeen ankers of potatoes and today I have commenced to my bere and expect to be done about Saturday. The expense is considerable. Have you finished?

Captain Sinclair leaves here this week for Whiteness to superintend the building of his house at Cova and will not be much more at Sandness. There is not now a person within half-a-mile with whom I can have a decent chat for five minutes. I will miss the Captain much.

Let me hear from you again as soon as you can, and with kindest love, your ever loving

Robert Jamieson

Sandness 14th July 1859

My dearest, darling love

It would seem that this is an age of likeness taking. Every person is now anxious "to see himself as others see him" and there is every reason to believe that the good old mirror which used to hang suspended on some conspicuous part of the apartment will be entirely superseded.

What do you think, we have had a photographer at Sandness! Such a personage and such a name never thought of visiting us or ever was heard of here before — it was entirely new and like every new thing created many conjectures and much excitement.

At first I did not think he would get any thing to do — the people looked on his art with something like suspicion. There was a secrecy, a darkness, a mystery about it which they could not fathom, and they ascribed it to the agency of Cloven Cloutie. "He doz it a' by da black art" they said and strange it is that in every place in the country where the photographer had been he found the same opinion prevailing. It is wonderful, but it has been the case in all ages, that every new thing, every thing which was not palpably evident to the senses, has been by the multitude ascribed to the powers of Satan.

After a day or two this feeling became considerably weakened, if not entirely radicated and there was a rage, a demand, a *mania* for likeness taking which was truly inspiriting. Married wives came dressed in their bridal attire, young lasses decked in their finest and best, married men in their Sunday's coat and with their Sunday's face and young lads with hair shining, sailor's tie and best and brawest jackets.

In a few cases young children were taken seated on their mother's knee and as it was impossible to make them sit still, more than one of them appeared with their hand shoved in their mouth, or busily engaged sucking the foot of their stocking. Families were taken in groups, in pairs and individually.

In general the likenesses were excellent and the photographer, Mr Goudie, would take and retake and take again until the individual was pleased. He stayed here and as I was anxious to understand the mysteries of his art, I may tell you — between ourselves — that for nearly a week I fear the boys did not receive much benefit. He is presently at Walls where he is taking likenesses by dozen.

I did not think I was near so ill looking till I saw my picture. I'm truly no bonny. I shall tell you what are regarded as its defects.

1st   One half of my shirt collar is invisible and the other half is brought prominently forward — quite in keeping with the slovenly habits of a bachelor.

2nd   The light was too intense and the consequence is that one of my eyes is shut and my features are twisted and drawn in an extraordinary manner, but as I have a book in my hand it looks as if I was in a "brown study".

I fear that it will cause you to lose all fancy for the original. You never yet sent me your likeness, think about it.

With kindest love,

your affectionate, loving Robert Jamieson

Gulberwick 3rd August 1859

Dearest Jamieson

I am very much obliged to you for sending the likeness for I wished to have it very much. I don't think it looks slovenly at all. I think it's very neat. You surely did not mean that I was not to shew it to any of our folk. I could not help that you know. I shewed it to each of them separately and father, mother, Maria, Eliza and John recognised it instantly. Thomas looked at it a while and then said "I think it's *something* like Mr Jamieson. It maybe is him. I'm sure it's him." Catherine looked at it for a long time and seemed very much puzzled then suddenly her face brightened up and she exclaimed "O, I ken! It's Mr Jamieson." I thought Bobby would have known it, but he did not. He said it was Magnie Tait.

You are not ill-looking. Neither are you – strictly speaking – handsome. You are just what I call good looking but you are noble, generous, loving and true. I love you very dearly indeed and would not give you for the handsomest man in the world.

So you want me to write more about Fanny Fern do you? I like real fun remarkably well, but I don't like *folly*. I for one am proud of Fanny and I intend to read all her writings. I don't believe that Elihu Burrit *can* write like her, but I should like very well to see his writings. You say that Fanny and Elihu would have made an excellent couple because they would have disputed and agreed, quarrelled and kissed. A pretty reason indeed. I hate your disputing and agreeing, quarrelling and kissing system. If ever I have a husband I shall let him know beforehand that I will have no quarrels with him, nor will I allow him to have any with me. If ever he attempts to quarrel he shall have it all to himself and "Quarrels we know may be often prevent, if only allowed but one side." Don't you think that is the wisest way?

Father was expecting a letter from you on Saturday. I wonder you never take any notice of his letters. It seems as if you never read them. Maria has taken the dorts. She says, "Doo daurna mention me whin doo writes him. For since he taks nae notice o' me, I dinna want ta tak any notice o' him. It's a pity that I should care sae muckle aboot him, since he cares sae little aboot me." She is of opinion that you have taken offence at something in one of her letters.

I have given up all hopes of seeing you now till after harvest, but you must come as soon as you possibly can. I hope the harvest will not be a long one. I have never looked at a French lesson since last year and at present I have very little time and as little heart for it. When you next come here we shall have a trial at it again. Please let me know how you get on with your Sabbath school.

But my paper is done so I must be done too and with kindest love

      will ever remain

        your loving Barbara L Laing.

Melby 10th September 1859

My dearest love

I am glad that the portrait reached you safely. Thomas and Catherine and Robert's difficulty in recognizing it was quite natural. Mr Craig maintained that it was James o'the Ha as they call him.

You will have heard of Mrs Peterson's insanity. I was much surprised when I heard it as I had seen her at Church only a few hours before in apparently good health. It would seem that her reason was dethroned in a moment. I am sorry for Mr Peterson as it is the greatest trial that ever befel him. Georgeson from Walls who was sent to Morningside last summer has returned as sober as a judge.

You have once or twice asked me if I had a sabbath evening school and I always forget to tell you – I have had once since the month of March and am beginning to like it remarkably well. At Whiteness I was not in raptures with it because I learned that it was more preaching that was required of me than school teaching. Here I do exactly what I think is best and no person interferes. I adopt the method I think best and as catechising is in my opinion by far the most profitable and interesting that is the very method I pursue. By catechising I do not mean repeating questions from a Catechism – I employ the term in its more comprehensive signification "to instruct by asking questions and correcting the answers" - and the consequence is that two hours in the sabbath school pass very quickly.

I am going to give you a very short epistle this time. With kindest love I am your loving

Robert Jamieson

Gulberwick 23rd September 1859

My dear Jamieson

We just finished shearing about half an hour ago and Maria threw our hooks over her shoulder. Hers fell with its point to the north east, Eliza's to the north and mine to the north west. Just as it should have done. Now don't think that I am superstitious. We merely did it for fun.

I was much pleased to learn that you had been keeping a Sabbath school for so long and liked it so well. I hear that Dr Scott is going to get married. Is it true? I have heard too that the Doctor has received a letter threatening that unless the schoolhouse at Sandness is properly repaired the school will be withdrawn. He will surely repair it.

Well Jamieson dear, your brother Willy has come at last and gone too. This forenoon just when I had got my work over and sat down to my seam there came a loud knock to the door. I was very glad you may be sure and welcomed him as heartily as I could. Father and Mother happened both to be in bed taking a nap. Father got up as soon as he was aware of Willy and very soon was talking away to him and both of them smoking. The little ones were soon good friends with him for he had such an inexhaustible store of sweeties and dealt them out so liberally. He only stayed with us about three hours. I was grievously disappointed for Maria and I had been planning to have a real merry night of it. But alas our glee was not to last long. But after all I'm thankfull that he came at all.

With kindest love, I am dearest Jamieson,

your loving Barbara

Sandness 7ᵗʰ October 1859

My dearest love

You will have heard of Dr Scott's wedding. It is no new occurrence but as it is the only thing that has happened since I came here worth mentioning I am sure you will excuse me for telling all about it.

During the doctor's residence at Melby this summer, scarcely a week passed without bringing him one, two and sometimes three lady visitors and as he is kind and generous and skilled in the art of pleasing, the consequence was that they felt very happy, were delighted with Melby and with every thing else. There were morning and evening walks along the sea shore, excursions to the Holm of Collaster, to Rangoon and elsewhere and thousands of opportunities of having a *tête-à-tête*, until at last the presence of the one became absolutely necessary to the happiness of the other.

I need not now tell you that the lady was Miss A.C. Watson and that after she left he became very dull, could find pleasure in nothing and often thought of writing and telling her all. Hearing one day that she intended going south by the steamer he resolved to accompany her and at once started for Reawick. Nothing was heard or thought of here until a few weeks after when the intelligence reached us that he and Miss Watson were to be married *instanter*. The news had but reached us a few days before he arrived at Melby.

I proclaimed him three times on the 2ⁿᵈ inst. and dispatched a man to Lerwick with the certificate at 5 o'clock AM on the 3ʳᵈ and as we are to have a regular d-e-m-o-n-s-t-r-a-t-i-o-n here on Tuesday I shall not conclude this my epistle till next week. So just one kiss – that's a darling. Now good night and may your dreams be ever of me.

13ᵗʰ: Such a day as was here on Tuesday no man living remembers. It is doubtful if such a day of rejoicing ever has been in the parish since the first Scandinavian in his fragile skiff crossed the Bay of St Magnus and landed on our shores. It was a 'high day'. Labour was suspended, every house was covered with flags, a cask of ale was landed from the "Hero" in the afternoon and a flowing bumper served out to all who chose to attend. Tar barrels were lighted, bon fires were kindled, shouts and shots were to be heard on all sides and all seemed to feel that it was the laird's wedding day.

The house of Melby was illuminated and at 8 o'clock a numerous hearty company sat down to tea in the parlour. There were thirteen gentlemen and fifteen ladies. We spent a *most* happy and harmoneous evening. There were toasts and sentiments and songs innumerable and will you believe it? Speeches, yes four speeches and I made my – now come don't laugh – my maiden essay. Such a night of hilarity, mirth, music and fun no Sandnessean ever witnessed in his native parish. We separated just as the cock's shrill clarion warned us of the approach of morn. I never spent a happier evening and all present declared the same.

I am thinking of coming East but as my crop is not yet in I do not like to leave it. From my very heart I wish that you were some miles nearer. Some dozen of miles farther West – I then could see you at any time and how dove like we would agree could I gain a glimpse of you once a month – as it is the distance is great.

I expect cards from the doctor on Monday – I shall not post this till I see if any come and shall let you see what like they are.

With kindest love,

Your ever loving Robert

Gulberwick 22nd October 1859

A thousand thanks, dearest Jamieson, for your last beautiful and welcome letter. You cannot imagine how happy it made me. I'm so glad you are coming; I'm only afraid it's too good news to be true. Oh Jamieson! I am in such a flutter I don't know what to say, but I just thought I would write to let you know how happy I was. Maria actually danced for joy and everybody is glad. We are all waiting to welcome you.

Sandness 24th October 1859

I had some thoughts of leaving home today, but the weather is unfavourable and as I intend going by Reawick from which a boat, I understand, goes to Scalloway every Thursday or Friday, I need not think of it again till next week.

Gulberwick 1st November 1859

It is now nearly three weeks since we heard that you were coming to see us and the news threw us all into a state of excitement from which we have never as yet recovered. I don't think Maria has been in her sober senses a single day since the news arrived. Almost every day she has a fit of dancing. And because we do not give expression to our feelings in the same boisterous way she says that we are a set of cold-hearted beings and that none of us have half as much regard for you as she does; but that's not true, for I am sure that nobody can like you any better than I do.

Almost every one of us has a different opinion about your coming here. Father professes that he does not expect you and yet he goes out every now and then and takes a sly peep up at the hill. Mother says that if you do not come it will be much against your will and she cannot believe that anything but illness would prevent you. Maria says she believes that you are cultivating a moustache and cannot make your appearance till it be fully grown. Eliza says it is so long since we

have seen you she believes that your hair has turned grey and you are afraid to show yourself, but if that is the case I shall not only love but reverence you.

Sandness 4th November 1859

I do hope that you will not be very offended – I ought to have written you last week, but I delayed in the expectation that this week I would be able to look eastward.

I told you some time ago that I had unfortunately caught a severe cold. I did not think it right then to say how ill I had been, but I may now mention that I was reduced to so much weakness that I could with difficulty walk a space of ten yards. Owing to the late harvest there was so much to be done outside that I could not have patience to stay within. It was not much I could do – if anything – but still I could not remain within doors and the consequence was that I caught cold afresh and when I received your last letter I was so unwell that I could not attempt leaving the house. I am much stronger yet I find it quite enough to walk from here to Melby.

Gulberwick 14th November 1859

I am very very sorry to hear that you have been so ill again. I knew that something was the matter that you did not come. I was bitterly disappointed but I deserved to be so. I should have treated you better when you were last here. I have often thought of your last visit and how chilled you must have felt when after coming such a distance to see me I received you so coldly. I can scarcely account to myself for my conduct at that time. You have forgiven me but I cannot forgive myself. I hope that your housekeeper is kind and attentive and takes care to do all in her power to make you comfortable. If so I shall feel myself her debtor.

Gulberwick 16th December 1859

My dearest Jamieson

I never came home from Lerwick till Tuesday night and have been so busy since that I never found time to write. As Mr Johnston's visit here is the all-engrossing topic of conversation with us at present, I shall at once proceed to give you a description of it as minutely as I can, being from home at the time, a circumstance which I very much regret.

I left home on a Tuesday and he came here on the Friday following. Maria and Eliza were in the byre and our John came to them and said there was a man and that he thought it must be Mr Johnston, for he was a little fat fellow and had a double lip. Father shook hands with him and said "so you've come at last." So they hurried and got their work done and in and tidied themselves and went *ben*. Maria says that he is not at all like what she fancied he would be, but much handsomer. She describes him as being rather short and stout, but on the whole very well proportioned, having a finely formed head, a noble brow, very fine blue eyes, a nose neither too large or too small and almost straight, a very pretty mouth, no double lip, but very red ones, a beard and moustache, not yet come to perfection but still very becoming and hair of a beautiful light brown colour. His voice she says is rather too soft for a man and his manner very reserved. He seldom spoke unless in reply to questions put to him.

Father and Maria sang a little to him and he, poor dear fellow, seemed to be much pleased with their endeavour to muse him. He could not be persuaded to stay over the Sunday, but he promised that if Father would come to Tresta for a night or two he would come here and stay two or three days. So we'll see.

I had a very pleasant visit to the town and staid just twice as long as I intended. I was at a Missionary meeting last Tuesday evening and enjoyed it very much. It was in the Methodist Chapel. There were half a dozen ministers on the platform and Mr William Sievewright was in the chair. There were several excellent speeches. The one I admired most was made by a young Methodist minister, but I don't know where he resides or how to spell his name.

Mr Duncan of Walls made the last speech. It was just a lot of humoursome rattle. I don't think he was ever intended for a minister. He neither looks or speaks like one and he's excessively vain. Father was at the meeting too, so you will likely see an account of it in the Ensign.

I am glad to hear that you have so many of your friends about you and that your housekeeper is such a nice person and keeps you all in such good order. I am particularly well pleased to hear that your sister and her little boy are with you. I had been thinking that if you had got a saddle and were well enough you might have come East and spent Christmas with us, but I fear that is out of the question.

So hoping to hear from you soon and that I shall be able to write you a better one next time I will conclude, and with kindest love, believe me ever to be, my dearest Jamieson,

Your loving Barbara Laing

Gulberwick 14th January 1860

A happy new year, dearest Jamieson.

I need not wish you a merry Christmas as that is past and I have learned from yourself that you have not had a merry Christmas. I am sorry for it but cannot help it. Had you been with us, you would have been merry enough.

We had a very nice time of it. Christmas eve was a very happy day with us. On Christmas morning Maria, Eliza and I got up at five o'clock and finished some presents which we had been preparing for the children. We spent an hour very pleasantly and then roused the children and gave them their presents. They were all very much surprised and delighted for we had kept the presents quite secret and when we saw them so pleased we felt amply repaid for our trouble. We found by experience that the surest way to find happiness was in trying to make others happy.

Father got up about seven o'clock when we had our breakfast. By the way Father has been in the finest humour all winter. After day break a while the report of a pistol announced the arrival of the Langton boys with our Christmas boxes so out we all went and bye and bye returned with our pockets full of sweeties.

Through the course of the day we had half a dozen gentlemen visitors. Two of them were married men, the other four young fellows just beginning to fancy themselves young men and very anxious to ingratiate themselves into the girls' favour.

During the afternoon we had Kitty Tait added to our number and we were all very soon on the most friendly terms. We spent the evening quite merrily amusing ourselves with fortune tellers, conversation cards, asking questions, choosing flowers, making up bouquets etc etc.

Oh I must not forget to tell you we have got a French master and he is such a queer fellow. I wish you were here. Father is making some progress but I have scarcely made any for, as the gentleman is a capital singer when he is in the house, I keep him singing. One of his songs is the queerest thing ever I heard. I should like you to hear it, but he will be away before you come here, unless you come very early in February.

Our soirée is the all engrossing topic of conversation here at present. I think it is a pity that it was not thought of sooner. It is now rather late in the season but as everybody seems to approve of the plan Father has determined to carry it into effect. Does it not seem strange that such a thing should be going to take place at Gulberwick? We must have you with us and the sooner you come the better. You tell me that it will be necessary for you to come and see me as you are forgetting now what like I am. I have never yet had my likeness taken or I would have sent it to refresh your memory, but let me tell you that you must not expect to find me so good looking as when you last saw me as it is now nearly sixteen months since and I am growing plainer as I grow older.

I wish you a happy new year and with kindest love will ever remain

    your fond loving

      Barbara L Laing

Melby 7th February 1860

I was delighted to hear, my dearest love, that your Christmas had been such a pleasant and such a happy one.

It may be the practice in some families, but your particular mode of distributing presents on Christmas morning is as a rule unknown in the Shetland Isles – at least I never heard it. The "W. W. World" was the first who told me of it. I think it an exquisitely delightful plan – productive of both pleasure, surprise and amusement. In the December number of Chambers Journal there is an article on Shetland marriages. It is well written but in several instances totally void of truth. The writer seems to have been present at some of them and if so he must be a very aged personage as the customs he describes cannot have existed in Shetland for the last 100 years. He represents us as a very primitive race. I have seen dozens of descriptions of Shetland but I have not yet seen a true one. They seem to have been written by strangers who had paid us a flying visit and the whole of them seem to be prejudiced. I had some thoughts of giving up Chambers and taking the "Leisure Hour" but as there is a tale promised I will continue it still.

I was truly surprised to hear that you had a French master, but that he was a living acting rational being did not enter my head. I thought it was a book – a volume of one of those literary weekly periodicals which profess to teach the language of Gaul – and as you spoke of not having it last February I believed that you only had the loan of it. How easy it is to arrive at an erroneous conclusion and to be utterly mistaken. No person unless he was plainly told could ever have conjectured that a French man or more correctly speaking a subject of Leopold was domiciled at Gulberwick. By what circumstance came Francois to live with you?

Is it really true – can it be possible that you are growing plainer as you grow older? Well it will just resolve itself into this – that when I see you I shall think you as beautiful as ever and were you as plain as you say you are I could love you none the less.

The opinions entertained respecting my not coming to Gulberwick last year are not quite correct. There is very likely the impression of a mousetrap, a moustache I mean, in the retina of Maria's eye and Eliza wants my hair to turn grey so that I may bear a resemblance, however small, to his elfin majesty, the fairy king, and to please her I shall make a wig of an old grey stocking which will answer famously well.

Various reasons contribute to prevent my being present at your soirée. This is not the most pleasant time of the year for traversing the deserts of mud and mire with which the Waster hills abound, although to do them justice they are neither so rough and rugged, bleak and bare, mossy and miry, sterile and stony as the Easter ones are. If anything can exist among them it must be fairies and one dark and rainy night, before Christmas a few years ago, I confess that I kept a strict out look on each side of me for them – this en passant.

My school is not yet examined. I have been expecting the minister for the last ten days, but as yet he has not come and owing to the unsettled state of the weather he cannot fix a day. Willy only commenced to Navigation the week before last and is anxious to acquire as much knowledge of it as he can before he goes South and were I to leave him in the midst of his perplexing angles he would not only be brought to a dead stand, but might think that I was somewhat careless.

Let me hear from you as soon as the soirée is over. With unfaltering love, your ever devoted

Robert Jamieson

Gulberwick 2nd March 1860

Well, Jamieson dear, our soirée is over and so pleased is everybody that all are wishing that we may soon have another. It was very well for a beginning. There were about seventy present, not including our own family. After tea was served, the song which Father composed for the occasion was sung and beautifully sung too I can tell you. Father then rose and made a speech, a very good one *I* thought, but I will not attempt to report it. There was no other speaker, so we and our friend Francois sung alternately for the greater part of the time.

I was not very well pleased with myself for I did not manage my part of the singing well. You know I cannot sing very high and I was afraid to pitch the tunes high lest I might not reach the high notes so I generally sung too low and I got excited too and actually broke down once or twice. After all I was very well pleased that you did not come for I was nervous enough, but had you been I should have been ten times worse.

After we had sung a number of pieces Father let us rest while he gave an address to the girls which though short was very nice and seemed to be well received.

I never saw such a pretty sight in the school before. The girls were all very neatly dressed and all looked so bright and happy. I thought my sister, Maria, decidedly the prettiest of the whole and she conducted herself so well I was proud of her.

A little before the company separated Robert Tait rose and made a few very appropriate remarks for which I felt very much obliged to him. We have had a busy time of it. Mr Saunders was here on Monday examining the school, our soirée was on Tuesday, notre ami Francois left us yesterday and tonight Mr Haworth has been here preaching.

I have been calling to mind the first few days you staid with us, how we longed for the evenings when our work done we could come and sit down and listen to you and Father conversing and telling stories. Then how very sorry we felt when you had to leave us and how very *very* dull we all felt after you had gone. It seemed as if part of our being had gone away with you. Yet I dreamed not then of loving you. I was quite astonished when I received the "Wide Wide World", but when the little card "I love thee" came I did not know what to think, could it really be possible that you loved me?

I would like to write more but I have not time. I hope to hear from you soon and shall wait patiently till you can come and see me. I hope that you have got your school examined now and that Willy is getting well on with his navigation.

So good bye and with kindest love I am,

your loving Barbara L Laing

Sandness 19th March 1860

My darling love

I was truly glad to hear that your soirée was such a harmonious one and fully came up to your anticipations.

Well, little Betsey Main after years of waiting is at last married. She is much the senior of her husband, but there may be no great harm in that. I was invited and went. We met at 4 o'clock, the minister came at five and that mysterious knot was tied at 6 pm. They were married in the capacious drawing room of the house of Melby and about forty persons young and old were present.

The duty of pulling off the glove was assigned to me so that I had a fine and full view of the whole. The company was a splendid one. I have not yet seen a better on any occasion of the kind. The bride was attired in a flowered lead coloured silk dress – around her neck was a plain white ribbon fastened in front with a large ivory brooch embossed with two reindeers – a marriage present I understand from Dr Scott. Her head was bare – her hair was formed in that peculiar fashion so common in Lerwick and the adjacent parishes but which only made its appearance in Sandness on 8th March 1860 and fastened behind with a rose in full blossom – to which a white ribbon was attached. Her maidens were similarly dressed and appeared to advantage. This is the first wedding at which I have been where those detestable caps did not disfigure otherwise good looking faces – I hope their reign is at an end. The dress of the men I need not describe – only that black coats, white vests and flaunting ties are as common here as they are any where. They were really a set of fine looking fellows and conducted themselves throughout with the utmost propriety and altho' the majority of them were sailors I did not hear the least offensive expression.

The dinner table which occupied the greater part of the dining room was laid out with taste and skill. The evening was spent most pleasantly. There were songs many and laughter much. I hope this will be the beginning of a thorough reform in our Sandness bridals which have hitherto been conducted on the erroneous principle of much expense and scant pleasure. Many are kept in poverty for years owing to the foolish expenditure of every shilling they possess on their weddings which not unfrequently lasts for three days. Brighter days I hope are dawning.

It was told me at Melby that you were receiving letters from a young man in Australia – that you were going south and that you were soon to be married and much of course I wondered thereat.

Now let me hear from you as soon as you can and with fondest love,

your loving Robert Jamieson

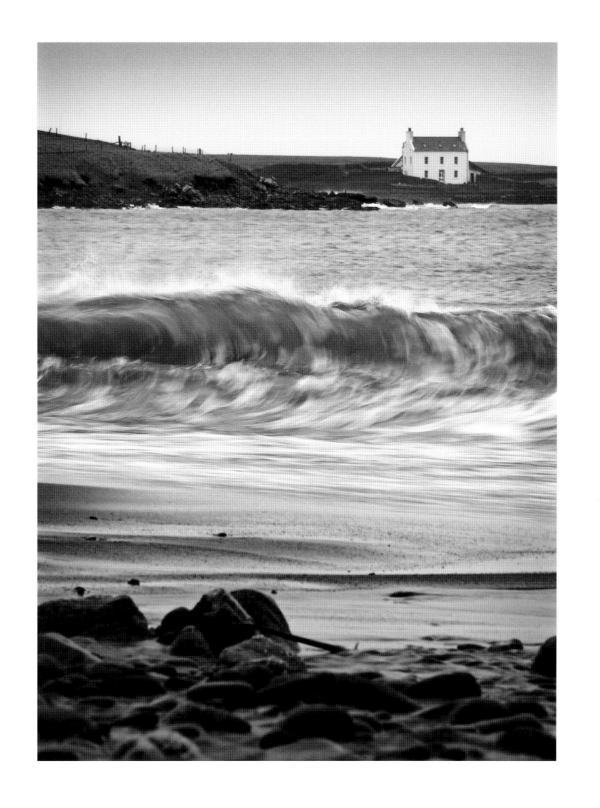

Sandness 26th March 1860

My darling love

I was truly glad that you were not so very offended at my non-appearance at your soirée – I could not come – it was not the fear of having to assist, or of making a speech that prevented me. To have made a speech in a strange parish and in a company of strangers is what I would not have liked and I knew well that you would never insist on my doing what I did not wish, and as for reading, if such were necessary – or reporting the whole proceedings, I should not only have complied willingly, but should have done it with pleasure.

I have now delved about an acre and an half of oats. I had intended to delve it about Christmas but there was so much to put to rights that I could not manage it. You think I could come East between the delving of my oats and bere. I could have done that very well, but I know that this is your busy season and it would be *awfu* lonely to remain in the house the whole day and you out – and you would be so weary at night that we could not have a protracted and agreeable chat. On the other hand you forget that I have a large field of potatoes to plant before we begin to the bere.

I was intending to come as soon as the voar was done, but it appears that your house is to be repaired about the same time. I must come however, even if nothing should be standing but the bare walls when I turn the corner of your hill. It would be quite romantic on a calm summer night to have a loving *tête-à-tête* in a roofless house, the blue ether our covering and the pale twinkling stars the witnesses of our harmony.

Small pox have broken out at Watsness, Walls and have spread during last week with alarming rapidity. It is only a few days since we heard it and there have been already nine cases and three deaths. They were brought from Aberdeen by a young girl who came home about a month ago and has since died. As her illness was only of a few days, those who have caught them were not aware of the nature of the disease – they thought it was inflamation and consequently took no precaution. I hope however that they will not spread further as the people will now be on their guard. The excitement is great – Watsness is between four and five miles from here and where the manse is situated. It is also said that small pox are in Weisdale.

Tell Mr Laing that the word 'aptata' has puzzled me terribly – I do not know the meaning of it unless it be the infinitive perfect, the passive voice, of the verb Apto – are – avi – atum – to fit, to accommodate, to adapt.

Now, come, you must write me once yet before I come East and with fondest love,

your loving Robert Jamieson

Gulberwick 21st April 1860

I had made up my mind not to write you again till you came here, but as you have not yet made your appearance I must just try it again. I am sick and tired of waiting. Now for two or three weeks Father has been expecting you and therefore he has not written. I have myself been looking for you this week. I was very sorry to hear that small pox had broken out so near you, I sincerely hope that they have not come to Sandness.

Would it not be better when you come here to take a passage to Scalloway if you could get it, as by doing so you would avoid coming through Walls, would be sooner here and not have so much fatigue. You surely will be here next week whatever way you come. I am going to Lerwick on Monday and will be there till I hear that you have come.

Father intends to commence repairing the school this week, but it will likely be two or three weeks before anything is done to the Gulberwick dwelling house.

Sandness 7th June 1860

There was a time, my darling love, when I found a peculiar pleasure in writing you at midnight when all was hushed and still, when nothing was to be heard but the dull hollow whistle of the vernal breeze. Why I should have preferred that particular hour is what I cannot explain even to myself.

Voar was finished on 18th May and peat casting about a week ago, (you I believe never saw a regular Shetland peat casting – it is nearly as good as a wedding and is worthy of a paper in "Chambers") and for a while at least there is something like a cessation from labor. I have now begun seriously to think of coming East and seeing you. If you could manage to post a note for me on Sunday evening stating when your house was to be repaired I would be glad.

I opened school about three weeks ago and the attendance at present is about 40. According to a promise made last year I expect that my school will be repaired in July. I will then have a week or two of liberty and it would be delightful to visit G-- during that delightful month.

Gulberwick 13th June 1860

Now, I am not a good letter writer and therefore ought not to criticise perhaps, but I do think that when people *can* write well they should do it. What a beautiful letter was your last to me! I might have known that it was written at mid-night, it was such a sleepy lifeless affair. It seems to me that you have been *noddin'* when you began to write, after writing the first page you have dropped asleep entirely. Just think of introducing a peat casting into a love letter. If you wished to let me know how they manage a peat casting at Sandness why not write a description of one, send it to "Chambers' Journal" and send to me the number in which it appeared? And then you tell me that you have *begun* to think *seriously* of coming East. Well, well!

Sandness 21st June 1860

I ought to apologise, dearest, for the very clumsy manner in which my last letter was expressed. I knew that it was utterly worthless when I sent it, but as the mountain tops had been already gilded by the orient beams of morn, I had not time to rewrite it. The introduction of a peat casting was truly ludicrous were it not that at these as well as at all other Shetland gatherings there is, or at least there appears to be, a good deal of love making.

Sandness 20ᵗʰ July 1860

My darling love

The reason why I did not come East at the time I mentioned was that on the Monday after I wrote you last I received intimation from the district Examiner of Registers that he would be here about the first of July. He came on the 6ᵗʰ, the day before, if my reckoning be correct, your house was deprived of its roof – and the weeks following I had to wait the arrival of instructions from him from Lerwick. I hope that by this time your house will be nearly finished and will prove fully more comfortable and will look amaist as well as new and shall feel obliged if you will have the kindness to tell me when you will be in a position to entertain strangers.

For the instruction of the readers of the Ensign you can tell your father that the fishing at Sandness and Papa was never so good in the memory of man. It is my opinion that nothing like it has ever been since the first boat was built in the parish. Some boats have taken as high as 20 scores or 4 cwt of ling for one trip – more she could not carry. Crops are rather aback.

It is not worth while to tell you that I have bought a boat – a beauty of a thing – and am now as keen on the fishing as I was on reading novels a few years ago. We take large hauls sometimes – James generally goes with me and we are as eager to have a pulling match with another boat as *boys* can be – and I don't think it does a particle of harm to either of us.

The Educational Institute, I think they call it, must be when completed a fine building and will I have no doubt prove a great benefit to the country – Lerwick is under great obligations to Mr Anderson and that penny subscription list was a proof that the Lerwegians are not ungrateful.

I am at no loss for newspapers. I have for the last twelve months received the "Illustrated News of the World" weekly – a superior paper. I also have the reading of an Edinburgh paper, the "Witness". I ordered the "John o'Groat Journal" when I saw that the "Ensign" had ceased to appear, as I should like to hear the result of that infamous poisoning case at West Burrafirth which has created much excitement for some time here. If you will have the kindness to continue the Ensign I will give it up. I was obliged by your sending the "Orkney Herald". It was the first copy of it I ever saw. I sent it to one of our class leaders and believe that it went to the parish. Mr Haworth was known here and the kindness of the Lerwegians to him was read with interest. I am at no loss for books either – I generally have more than I can read – scarcely a new book enters the parish that does not find its way here, and I still take "Chambers".

Let me hear from you as soon as you can. Forget not to tell me when your house is again set in order and with kindest love,

I am your truly affect.

Robert Jamieson

Gulberwick 21ˢᵗ July 1860

Dearest Jamieson

Since you did not come the week that you intended it is just as well you did not come at all for we got lime sooner than we expected. The work commenced just a week after I wrote you and the roof was taken off the butt end of the house on Johnsmas morning before breakfast, and we have all been crowded into the ben end since. The roof is still on the closet so the children still sleep there, but Maria and Eliza and I sleep ben. If you could get a peep at us some night after we have gone to sleep, you would think it funny to see us lying one here and another there about the floor rolled in rugs. We are of course subjected to a great deal of inconvenience, but then there is so much fun about it and that makes up for the inconvenience.

The mother of Maria's lover – and indeed all his friends – are very anxious to further the courtship and they have several times asked Father to allow Maria and me to come and spend an evening with them, so we went in on Wednesday and a very pleasant evening we spent. They are all very fond of music. Alick and his brother can sing bass beautifully and play on the violin and their youngest sister has a very sweet voice, so we spent the greater part of the time in singing. I never sang better or Maria either. We seemed just to have got into the spirit of it, and the time passed so pleasantly that we felt sorry when we had to leave. They were exceedingly kind and invited us to come whenever we could and stay as long as we liked. Alick and two of his sisters came more than half way home with us.

My position is so uncomfortable that I cannot write any more. I am perched upon a high bed in the school writing on a box. This is a funny time if it would not rain so. It does look as if I was never to see you again. There is always something coming in the way.

30ᵗʰ July   Now for three mails I have been looking for word from you, but have got none. When it comes I suppose it will be full of excuses and pleadings for pardon as usual.

Since I last wrote everything here has been turned topsy turvy. The school has been roofed and we are living in it. Our own house is roofless and we are working at it. I say *we* for this is a work in which we all have to lend a hand. I hope that it too will be roofed by Lammas. But I don't know for the work is progressing rather slowly. Father is working like a slave both body and mind, pointing and whitewashing the inside of the schoolroom, and when that is done it will look better than ever it did before, but it will be long before our own house will even look so well as it did before, as means cannot be raised to get it lofted. I wish for his sake that the work was done. We are quite happy and comfortable in the school and our dear little friend Elizabeth Malcolmson is with us as she says "enjoying the fun of the thing".

I wish you could have been with us too, it would have been delightful. You would have charming company, for here are "Maidens fair with garlands crowned". We all wear garlands now. Maria is very expert at making them and busy tho' we are she finds time now and then to weave some. What tho' there be sunburnt faces, scratched hands and bare and dust soiled feet? These along with bright eyes and rosy cheeks (of which there are plenty here) are all tokens of health and industry, and instead of diminishing only add to our charm. Oh you have no such society at Sandness.

Now good bye for the present and with kindest love,

your loving Barbara L Laing

Sandness 27th August 1860

This I see will never do, darling, I have been waiting to hear from you and I daresay you have been expecting me to reply to your last letter which is nothing more than I should do. Lammas has past and I am anxious to know if your house be finished. Now that the nights have become long, cold, dark and damp, I fear that the romance as well as the fun of the thing will be getting nigh over – that is if your domicile be still *minus* the roof – and that you will now be on the confines of stern realities. You do peep into the ideal occasionally I see.

I should have been well pleased to have seen you crowned with garlands – I'm not so sure about the torn hands and bleeding feet – and to have been in the midst of such a laughing blooming circle.

You seem to be delighted with the present state of things and to commiserate my life of isolation at Sandness – you say truly that I have no such company as you have. I never was so much alone – I have neither company nor companion – a chat worthy of the name is now a thing of the past – months pass without my coming in contact with a person who understands the rudiments of our language. It is more than a year since I was out of the parish – I visit none and receive no visitors. You are my only, my sole correspondent and the principal intelligence which reaches me is conveyed through the columns of a newspaper. Such a hermit life I daresay you think is insupportable. On the contrary. I was never better and seldom happier. I now take pleasure in what I found none before and fully believe that every place as well as every situation of life has its own particular enjoyments.

In a few weeks now we will be quite busy. Write me as soon as you can and forget not to tell me if your house be finished

With fondest love, your ever affectionate Robert Jamieson

Gulberwick 29th September 1860

Dearest Jamieson

I do not believe that I could live without writing to you and hearing from you. My birthday is tomorrow week and oh! how happy I would be if you could be here, but I scarcely dare hope to see you so soon as that, the harvest being such a late one. It is very nearly two years since you were here last.

I have some good news to tell you. An old scholar of Father's who has a very great regard for him has sent a handsome subscription for the school and a present to Father and a very nice letter along with it. We really ought to be thankful to Providence for sending this timely aid. Had it not come we should have had a cold winter of it for want of a loft above the ben room, but we will soon have it now. The schoolroom is now quite finished and it really looks a great deal better and is far more comfortable.

We finished shearing our bere yesterday, nearly a week later than we finished the oats last year. We will have some oats for shearing soon, but the greater part of it is still very green. I hope you are getting well on with yours. I hope either to see you or hear from you by next Saturday. You must come if possible.

So good bye for the present and with kindest love, I am dearest Jamieson your truly loving

Barbara

Melby 4th October 1860

At present, darling, I have only time to send you a very few lines. I see that I will not be able to be with you on your birthday as I thought I might be. I have this evening finished shearing my bere. It is a heavy crop and as I have been compelled to cut it down green it will require much care, especially in such weather, to cure it properly. My oats are still far from being ripe, but down it must come next week. Much depends on the weather which at present is most inclement. As soon as my oats are in sheaves I shall if well come East. I shall leave the delving of the potatoes to those at home. You must not regard this as a letter. I am just about as busy as I can be.

7th October 1860

Allow me to congratulate you, dearest, on the anniversary of your birth. I know not how many good wishes I shall send you and I am nearly at a loss how or in what form to express them. De Lamartine mentions an Italian friend who in his younger days not only gave up writing but often remained silent because he found language an entirely insufficient medium for the full and free expression of his thoughts. To wish for you everything that is good and excellent does not seem enough.

Margaret Tait was to contract last night with a young man called William Bolt whose father, a blacksmith, removed from Twageos to Sandness in 1840. William is the only young man of literary tastes in the parish and is about twenty-three years, but the daughter of one of our elders considers that she has a claim upon him. How he will manage I don't know. Very likely the marriage will be postponed.

15th October 1860

Last week was a very busy one. I had cut down about thirty-four thraves of oats. I was afraid of snow, of hail and was anxious. I had from three to six shearers every day, they complain bitterly of the corn being 'Kegled'. Find that word in the dictionary if you can. Seven shearers came this morning. Had it kept dry I would have nearly finished. Bad day this.

Gulberwick 19th October 1860

This is desperate weather and the harvest is never like to come to an end. When the weather is good I like harvest better than any other season of the year but this one has been every thing but pleasant. It's a mercy we have something else to think about.

Our loft is being laid and we are to have our Hallowevens' banquet up stairs. It will be a nice snug comfortable little place when it is finished. You could not stand in it with your hat on, it is so low, but it will do very well, and when Father is done I am going to undertake the trimming of it and I shall make it a little beauty.

And so Margaret Tait is going to marry, I think she would better not, since any other body has a claim on her lover. As for Mr Burgess, I have not heard anything about him for some time, nor do I want to hear for I think him a precious scoundrel.

O, Jamieson, I wish you were come, I long to lay my head on your shoulder and have a nice little talk.

Sandness 21ˢᵗ November 1860

My darling love

I only reached home last night – I have felt dull and lonely ever since I tore myself from you and this morning I am particularly so. How I wish I had only been leaving home to see you. Those eight days I spent with you appear as a dream, I was so happy, so delighted. It was so unlike anything I have experienced during the last two years, that I can scarcely persuade myself that I have been anywhere but in the regions of fancy.

Once from you I was very anxious to reach home. Mr Goudie offered me his horse to take to Sandness. I accepted him gladly but had to leave him at Cova. Saturday was a very cold day and Captain Sinclair enticed me to stay till Sunday, believing that the weather would become milder. On Sabbath the weather was more inclement still and the roads were too frosty to proceed any other way than on foot. Went to Clousta on Monday and took a boat from there to Sandness yesterday. A distance of twelve miles. I had to bribe the lazy fellow of a boatman with extra fare before I could make him move. He thought it so cold and a part of the voe was frozen. I don't think his wife's face had been washed since January. She was a darky.

Remember me very kindly to Maria and I hope that ARW will declare himself frankly. At present he seems a sort of milk and water wooer. It is difficult to know whether he means anything or nothing. If I thought he meant anything I would reply to his letters in a very friendly, fraternal manner. If on the other hand I thought him as a mere cake and pudding suitor I would supply him with a little pepper.

My visit to you has made "single blessedness" blessedness no longer. I cannot be happy without you. During the last two years I have planned and schemed – done every thing in my power to get things put in order and considering how very little I had when I came here, I have succeeded beyond my expectations. It has cost me many a thoughtful hour, but I preferred to struggle alone rather than lead you into embarrassments. My house, as I told you is not as good as I would like. I now regard the battle as fought and as I mentioned to you when I was East, I do not think there is any use in waiting much longer.

Winter is an unfavourable season, but I am perfectly willing that we should marry in summer. Are you willing? I should like to you to be plain. Tell me freely.

Now, dearest, let me hear from you. I am longing, *longing* much.

Your devoted,

Robert Jamieson

Gulberwick 25th November 1860

My dear dear Jamieson

You wish me to be plain. So I will. I am quite willing to marry in summer, if I can be ready by any possible means, and I am even willing that it should be in May if that would be most convenient for you. I weary for you quite as much as you can do for me and I love you with my whole heart. You need not mind the house for me for I have been used to a good deal of discomfort.

Already it seems to be a long time since you left us. For my part I always felt happy when you were here but I never before enjoyed a visit from you so intensely. I cannot tell you how happy I was while you staid and how unwilling I felt to let you go. Well, well! I did not discover till this moment that I had begun on the wrong side of the paper, what an awkward mistake! Please excuse me. I am very glad to learn that you are nothing the worse of your jaunt. And so Uncle Lawrence took you up to tea. Mother was in town yesterday and Aunty told her all about it and told her that they were all highly pleased with you. She tells me that I must not let another summer pass and assures me that she shall do her best to bake a good cake for my wedding.

I forgot to tell you in my last that your beloved brother Kennedy has been one of the most noted revivalists in the north of Ireland. What do you think of that? He has received some sort of a testimonial for his great services and he sent the paper in which it appeared to Mr Sloane.

The church bell is ringing so I must be done for this time.

With fondest love, your affectionate Barbara

Sandness 5th December 1860

My dearest darling love

This is a very quiet evening. As in duty bound I went to the muckle kirk in the morning. In the afternoon I went to the Methodist chapel to hear the clergyman who has been lately appointed to the Walls district. He is quite a young man, pale and worn with thought.

He does not enter the pulpit with the measured solemn step of the venerable clergyman, there is a lightness and gaity in his manners. He is a long time in selecting the hymn and turns over the leaves of the hymn books with the air of a young schoolmaster in selecting a pleasant but instructive lesson for his pupils and telling them at the same time that it is most excellent and he is sure that they are all very nice children, and will read it to perfection, and feel highly gratified. He kept up the attention of his audience for half an hour. I was interested. Unless I am mistaken he will be highly popular here. From his accent he seems to be a native of London, he has such words as "h – even", "h – enemies".

I have been told that the Procurator Fiscal would be glad to discover Kennedy's whereabouts. He was capable of anything and one cannot but view any movement whatever with suspicion in which men like him are regarded as chief actors.

My wedding day was one which I always liked to envelope in the mist of the future. I never was fond of thinking of it as being very near. My sentiments are now entirely changed and I should be happy to know the particular day on which we are to be married. Resolve and let me know.

With just one kiss from your ever loving Robert Jamieson

Lerwick 13th December 1860

My dearest Jamieson

I am so glad, I have seen Willy and spoken with him too. I had been feeling very dull all the day before, but I was as merry as a lark after I saw him. I shall like him extremely well for a brother in law. He resembles you very much some ways, for one thing he has the very way of saying "oh yes, yes" that you do. The dear kind fellow went and bought some sweeties. He has a kindly face and a merry laugh.

My Uncle, who was present at Mr Hunter's lecture on "Enthusiasm", said that it was a very good one to those who could understand it, but they were few and there was too much "show off" he said. What an immense amount one might find to say on a subject like that. All his examples and illustrations were drawn from Ancient History which of course very few of his audience were acquainted with. The object of the lecture seemed to be more to show off his own learning than to benefit his audience. Dr Spence lectured last Friday night on "Fire" and a very instructive and interesting lecture he gave I hear. The Doctor's manner is exceedingly easy and agreeable they say and there is no such thing as showing off with him. He never speaks on any subject but what he is thoroughly acquainted with.

I never had a more pleasant visit to the town but I would like to be home now and, if spared, I shall write again from there.

22nd December   I came home on Monday night with Maria. As soon as we opened the door we were met by all the children, and then there was such a round of kissing to be gone through it was some time before I got farther than the door. Little Bobby actually danced for joy, he really surprised me, and then everyone had some thing new to tell. Eliza had learned to milk the cow, John had been at Lerwick with

Father, Thomas had wrought the whole rule of subtraction in one night and this he seemed to think was a most remarkable performance. Catherine had knitten a whole pair of stockings for herself. Kitty Tait had learned to knit the "French purse" and many more things they had to tell. It is very nice to come home after being away a while.

Today is Father's birthday. He is forty nine years old but he looks much older and no wonder, he has gone through so much.

I shall bid you goodbye for the present and wishing you a merry Christmas and a happy new year

I am, dearest Jamieson,

Your loving Barbara

Lerwick 14th January 1861

I wonder what *can* be the matter, dearest Jamieson. You had no shirts to make that must be finished before Christmas, no nightcaps to make for sick babies and nothing in the world could prevent you from catching the post.

I came to town and have been since. My aunt has been very poorly almost all the time I have been in. If I was a married woman and had a husband like my uncle I think I would like to be ill now and then for sake of the petting. Uncle just adores Aunty. He waits on her night and day, tries to anticipate every wish, speaks to her in the kindest manner possible and never is happy till he gets her well again. There are very few husbands like Uncle.

One day I had occasion to be in ARW's shop. He handed me a parcel neatly made up and addressed to me. When I came home I found it contained a copy of the Scottish Temperance League register for 1861. Maria took it and began to look over the names of the members of the League and to my great astonishment she found my name among them. ARW had never so much as asked me if I would like to be a member of the League so it looked very odd. I believe that the poor fellow meant it as a pleasant surprise, thinking that I, like some others, would be very much gratified to see my name in print, great fool!   This with one or two other little things has had the effect of convincing father and mother that it was me he was in love with and not Maria. Still I believe nothing of the kind myself. My cousin Arthur insists that ARW was in love with me and that I encouraged him and he gives me such lectures on flirting. Of course the Lerwick girls are terrible flirts.

Jenny Johnston shew me a new years gift which she had got, the prettiest thing I ever saw. It is a bible beautifully bound in mauve silk velvet with a handsome case to keep it in too. I saw the note which accompanied it. It was not what one might have expected to have accompanied such a gift. It was badly written and miserably spelt. Jenny said it was from a sailor lad and I believe her for none but a sailor would have thought of giving Jenny such a gift. He only called himself a "well wishing friend" but he must be more than a friend. Aunty was thinking it was Willy, but I don't believe that, Willy has more sense.

I send a copy of Longfellow's pretty new poem for you to see and tell me what you think of it. It is long past twelve and I can hardly hold up my eyes so I shall have to give in.

With kindest love,

Barbara Laing

Sandness 18th January 1861

Well, my darling, I really believe that I shall become dreadfully jealous of you after all. You will be sure to make me so. I wonder at you. Do you think that I have a heart of stone – insensible to every emotion? Rocks, I believe, could be melted and I know that they can be moved and surely I cannot be more incapable than they. To tell me with as much coolness as if it was a matter of no importance whatever that another was in love with you is more than human nature can bear. Did I say become? I am as jealous as I can stand and no marvel. He is a funny creature yon. I wonder if he would drown ... I'll wager he is amphibious and if he would volunteer to march over the piers it would be a relief and it would not hurt him in the least.

Who would ever have thought it? Where in all the world shall I find another sweetheart now? How uncertain is every thing human! I have been indulging in the hope that my courting days were drawing near a close, but I am as far from it as ever. I shall have to begin anew and how I loved, how adored her! She was dearer to me than life. I shall never suppose so much trust again. But why soliloquise?

I had not only to institute an inquiry, but personally examine the individuals in company with the young woman who died on the hills of Kellister on the evening of the 22nd December and report to the Pro. Fiscal. The first communication of an official nature I ever had with him and I sincerely hope it will be the last.

Willy came home on Monday evening and says Jenny was showing him the bible she had received as a present from her "sailor lad" and you were right in believing that he did not give it. As Andrew Jamieson was in Lerwick the week before Christmas, you may regard him as the generous sailor. He and she are corresponding regularly. He left Snarraness and came home to his father with the intention of coming to school, but he has been so unwell during the winter that he has not come. He tells me that he admires Jenny. Is not that good?

I shall be happy to hear from you and give me a full description of the wedding. I will then see what like they are to the weddings here. That lecture of Mr Brown's was absurd nonsense. He knows as much about Shetland as a cat.

I do not like to say much about it, but the insertion of your name in the STL register without your consent was very absurd.

Excuse this hurried note, written with a *quill*,

your ever loving

Robert Jamieson

Gulberwick 23rd January 1861

Dearest Jamieson

I shall according to promise proceed to give you a description of the wedding of Mary Henderson and Willy Linklater.

We were told to come at eight o'clock in the morning and to be sure and not come later. When we reached the house the breakfast was ready and the greater part of the guests had arrived and were seated. Colin, who was best man, took Maria and Kitty Tait and me and placed us in a nice quiet corner and came himself and waited on us, so we thought ourselves very well served I can tell you. Colin tried to talk to us but it was the next thing to impossible for us to hear him. Such a noise! Everybody was speaking and all at the same time, so I was completely dumbfoundered.

After breakfast was over the bride and bridesmaidens all went to dress. The bride had a poplin dress with broad stripes of purple and grey, a blonde cap and a white plaid with a coloured border. The bridesmaidens had some blue, some grey and some brown dresses, but they all had light shawls and blonde caps. Caps you know are considered indispensable here so Maria and I could not be singular we had caps too. After the dressing was done, the procession was formed and we left for Lerwick. There were sixteen couples of us in all and we made a fine show.

When we came to the manse Mr Saunders himself received us at the door and conducted us to the drawing room. He did not make the ceremony very long and I liked his manner very much. He remarked that this was the first couple from Gulberwick whom he had had the pleasure of uniting.

We came home between two and three. The company waited some time outside expecting them to come and throw the cake over the bride's head (an old custom which I do not know the meaning of) but no cake was thrown. Then came dinner. If there was noise at breakfast there was more now. It was perfectly deafning and the quantity of bread and mutton devoured was astonishing.

After dinner some of the young folks wanted to send for a fiddler. Now the bride's father died in harvest, so she did not consider it consistent to have a fiddler at the wedding and put a stop to it immediately. As soon as that was decided Maria tried to set agoing some games. She tried several but none of them seemed to take till she tried the American Post. This seemed to meet with general favour and when once it was set agoing they would never stop. Andrew, Maria's partner, said that he never got so many kisses in all his life before; and he might never have the chance again so he wanted to take all he could get. The whole night from teatime till suppertime was spent playing the American Post, so you may imagine what a number of letters must have been delivered during that time.

One thing that astonished me very much was the quantity of spirits that the men drunk. I never thought that any man could drink so much and yet be able to keep his feet. I'm sure that all there drank two or three gills and some far more.

We came home as soon as supper was over which was between eleven and twelve but all the rest staid to sleep in the barn. From what I have heard they did not have a very comfortable night of it. I enjoyed myself better than I expected but still I would not like to have a wedding like that.

With fondest love,

your affectionate Barbara Laing

My dearest love,

This has been a play day with me – my school was examined yesterday and I intended to spend the whole day and the entire night in letter writing, but I have done nothing. I was not feeling well on Sabbath morning, but to church I had to go as I had a duty to perform. The cold was intense, the service rather long, the countenances of every person was of a bluish tinge, and to crown all we had to walk home in the rain. Every person is complaining. The minister was here on Sabbath night. I have not had a comfortable chat since he was here last and what was equally strange he tells me the same tale. He studies astronomy and geology and his mode of conveying information is graphic and as it is impossible for limited intelligence to remain always aiming at the stellar orbis, or the formations of this earth of ours, it was necessary to introduce occasionally some other topic and thus the evening passed pleasantly enough. Ministers might convey a great deal more information in their sermons than they do and if they would only set about it I for one would listen better.

We were thatching the school, one of the lads was standing on a ladder. The space between the ladders and the wall suggested to the foolish boy Bobby the idea of a door and he was running through it when a stone from the top of the wall fell on his head and cut it to the bone. The stone was a large one and it was a marvel he was not killed on the spot. He bled profusely.

I sent an express for an individual who professes to have much skill both as a surgeon and a physician. He came, examined the wound, dressed it, instructed me how to manage it and told me that had it been in his crown it would have been very dangerous as it would have cut the nerves which run from there to all parts of the body. "A lad east of here" he said "fell and cut six nerves in the quarle

of his crown". He saw them. That poor fellow's nervous system must have been literally unstrung. Bobby is running about again. He is not so lively as he was and is as pale as a sheet. I hope however that he will soon be quite well. His escape was a very narrow one.

I have received Mr Laurenson's letter and shall reply to it soon. I think I will be able to furnish him with a few trow stories. Some years ago these stories were very common over all the country. It was in fact the only fireside literature and often have I listened to them with wonder and awe, was afraid to move beyond the threshold that I was conveyed to some gorgeous subterranean appartment, but the generation who believed in them and delighted most in relating them has passed away.

Willy is very well, little Bobby is labouring away in the hooping cough and big Bobby is brawly.

With fondest love, your ever loving

Robert Jamieson

Sandness 8ᵗʰ April 1861

I have not yet "made up my mind", darling, whether I will go to Lerwick with the enumerations books or will I send them. Sometimes I think I will go – at other times I think I will not. This is an awkward season for leaving home and it is such a horrid long tramp.

I have written Mr Rannie and if he go I will have to follow. If he remain I will stand as good a chance as he. We may either deliver the books personally or send them, but the sheriff has ordered us to attend personally and it may not do to refuse. All, however, we have to do in town is not worth to take us so far and many of the registrars I am sure cannot attend. We have been busy all day and have not yet completed our returns – it will take us the greater part of tomorrow.

11ᵗʰ April: Last week I was too ill to write, having caught a most severe attack of influenza and this week I have been so busy. I cannot say as yet whether I will be in town about the census. I have received a circular from the sheriff clerk tonight and Tuesday the 23ʳᵈ is the day fixed for all the registrars in Zetland to appear at the sheriff's clerk's office. A "prime lot" they surely will be, but it is doubtful if they all can attend. I will however be able to tell you on Monday whether I will be among the number present.

Willy and Jacob and Jamie leave here on Saturday week for the South. They will ship for Quebec, Jacob at 15/– per month and Jamie at £2.10/–. Willy does not say. Before I need write to them I hope you will be here.

I am ashamed to send you this and yet I cannot help it.

With fondest love, your ever loving R Jamieson

Gulberwick 30ᵗʰ April 1861

My dear dear Jamieson

I hope that you are now safely at home, not tired in the least and have found everything there going on as well as if you had never been away. I am dreadfully lonely, but I comfort myself with thinking that next time you come I shall go with you. I know I can never make as good a wife as you deserve, but since you have chosen me I shall try to do the best I can and oh how happy I shall be if I can only make you happy. If I only succeed in this I shall ask nothing more.

Mother did not give you any direct answer when you spoke to her on Sunday, but you need have no doubt of her willingness. She has frequently said to Maria that she knew of no person to whom she could so readily entrust my happiness. As for father I know that he approved of it from first and would have had no objections had we married six weeks after we first began to correspond, but still you will have to write to him. It is a mere matter of form but it might be taken as a slight if you did not.

I think we will finish the voar about the end of next week, and then I shall begin in earnest to make my preparations.

I am dearest,

Your loving Barbara

Gulberwick 18ᵗʰ May 1861

My dearest Jamieson

Thanks for your last sweet letter. It was a beautiful one, something like the first ones. I have not been very well this week but have managed to accomplish a good deal of work. I have not done much for myself, but I have finished the greater part of the work I had in. Mother was in Lerwick on Tuesday and uncle gave her a sight of the merino and she says it is a lovely colour and a real good quality. She did not see the cloak but uncle said that it had come too. They are going to keep it till I come in myself, but I must hear from you again before I can.

About things you require. I would like to get a white shirt, a particularly nice one. I do not know the classical name of the woollen stuff. I would just call it either coloured flannel or flannel shirting. I would like to make that myself. About the gloves, unless you can tell me the number that fits you I cannot get them, but you could get them when you come East and the neck tie, I can get that. For my own things I require a bonnet, cloak, gloves and lining and trimming for the merino dress. For these things it will require upwards of a pound if you have it, well if not I will get a loan of it from mother till you can send it for I will not take my wedding things on credit from anybody either on your name or my own. If you do lend the money do not bother with an order, just send it in a letter. The white dress will have to be dispensed with. I would have liked it especially as you seemed so anxious to have it, but I cannot get it myself by any means and you, I am perfectly sure, have more to do than you will manage so we must not think about it.

I would rather anything than write about all this. It is extremely disagreeable but I can't help it. I heartily wish it was all over. I used to think that wedding preparations must be very delightful to the parties concerned but I do not find it so. I wish I were safe at Sandness with you and the vexatious preparations over.

You must excuse this dearest. It is a poor return for your lovely one.

With fondest love,

Your devoted Barbara

Sandness 23ʳᵈ May 1861

It seems, dearest, that you are now immersed in the practical. I'll tell you, return whatever work you have on hand belonging to other people and let them make it for themselves. Such incessant application to the needle must be injurious.

I finished delving last week but we are still in a state of confusion. So much remains to be done. Both my servants came on Monday. It is unfortunate that the Registrars of Burra, Weisdale etc should have made such a mistake in their census returns – according to them education is at a very low attitude in those parishes. It has been a misunderstanding with them, poor fellows, and any explanation they can give is now too late.

I am glad to hear that your merino and cloak have come. Your plan of purchasing with ready money is such a very excellent one that if persevered in through life it will make us if not rich at least independent and as a reward for adopting such a noble resolution I herewith enclose you a 20/- note. Let me know if it reaches you safely.

With fondest love, your loving

Robert Jamieson

Gulberwick 24th May 1861, the Queen's birthday

My dearest Jamieson

Summer has come now in reality and the fields are all covered with flowers. The banks and burnsides are almost white with daisies and primroses and everything is looking fresh and beautiful. Gulberwick will be in its glory when next you see it. Do you know I never thought our little valley half so pretty as now that I am thinking of leaving it.

I used to think when reading or hearing of the emotions some people felt on leaving their native place, "well I'm sure I will not feel anything like that when I leave Gulberwick," but now that I am really going to leave it I do feel a little. The sand, the rocks, the banks, the burnside all have sunny memories and pleasant associations connected with them.

When children, among the rocks used to be sort of fairy land to us peopled by the most charming beings imaginable whom we used to visit now and then and talk with most lovingly. And we ourselves were very grand personages. Our cotton frocks were the costliest silk, our bare feet were shod with stockings of silk and boots of satin lined with the softest fur and our little brown hands and arms were adorned with the richest jewels and I never saw anybody so beautiful as we fancied ourselves, or so good either. Oh! How happy we were then. What castles we built and what lovely pictures we painted. Sometimes we do still. I've just been painting some lovely little pictures and building some pretty airy little castles. It is a very pleasant employment and quite harmless. I could not do them justice or I might give you a description of some of my castles and pictures.

I am all alone, the rest are all in the school and I am left to take care of the house and the cows. I have been reading "Good Words" the whole day and am now rather tired tho it is such a luxury. I have been reading about St Columba and General Havelock and several pieces of beautiful poetry. There is no kind of reading I like better than fine poetry and the lives of great and good men. Perhaps it is not right but I like it far better than listening to sermons, unless indeed the preacher be like Mr Haworth. Some Sunday when we are at home together perhaps you will again read over the papers that interested you.

When you were here I told you that I could not sing any and indeed I had my private doubts whether I would ever be able to sing again, but I am happy to tell you I was mistaken for I have been carolling away this week as merrily as the larks.

I must stitch away till I come West and then I am going to make stockings for you. It will be a very pleasant change. I have a number of pretty little plans to put into execution when I come West but I'm not going to tell you them yet. There is a great contest among the children who is to go home with me. John says he would like to go and Thomas says that where I go he will go and Katy calmly tells them that neither of them need think about it for she is really going.

They all send their kind love to you and with fondest love,

believe me ever to be affect.

Barbara

Sandness 2ⁿᵈ June 1861

When I tell you, dearest, that yesterday was our peat casting and that the whole week previously was one of preparation you will perhaps excuse me for not writing you by last post.

It would occupy too much space and at the same time be so entirely unseemly to give a description of such a prosaic affair "in what should be a love letter" that I cannot think of doing it. I shall however on some quiet evening give you a very minute verbal description, so that next year if all be well you shall know how to superintend the whole matter and if you do not join me in expressing a feeling of hearty relief when all is over I am much mistaken.

I can fully enter into your feelings and sympathize with you on your prospect of leaving Gulberwick. To cross the country is to every person an arduous task and not only the journey itself, but several circumstances may combine to prevent you visiting your friends at Gulberwick except at rare intervals.

It may happen that years may elapse between your visits. But I shall hope that in a very short time you will become a genuine Sandnespian. The people are rather a rough outspoken race but are really kind-hearted and obliging and I feel assured that in a short time they will both esteem and respect you and although Sandness by many may be regarded as lonely, yet we will try to find amusement and will learn to depend on our own resources.

I enclose you an order on R. Sinclair & Co. I have written to Mr Sinclair. You need have no hesitation in presenting it – they will supply you. As I seldom wear white shirts and do not care about them you need not go to a very high price for one. I should like the woollen shirt to be a neat pattern (not tartan) and as for the neck tie you can please yourself. And let me not forget there are gloves –

gloves for each of us – and very likely something more. You must be particular and tell me what you require.

Let me know when you are getting ready and how you like your dress and cloak. By the bye there is one thing which I have always been intending to write you about but have always forgotten – namely a ring. I do not know the size of your finger – it is not likely I will meet you in Lerwick and I should like to buy it myself. I expect either Jamieson or Hicks has them. Have you any old ring – any sort of thing or a brass one which you would send me and which is the exact size of your finger? Or can you suggest any other way I could procure one of the exact size?

I think of you incessantly and love you devotedly.

RJ

Gulberwick 10th June 1861

My dearest Jamieson

Since we first began to correspond, I have always regarded Sandness as my future home. I love Gulberwick, yes, and always will love it, but it is Sandness that is associated in my mind with the future and then just to fancy my wearying with you, my husband, no, no. Banish the idea I beseech you. What is the use of making yourself uncomfortable by dreading an evil that will never come to pass, but enough of this.

I went to Mr Sinclair's, met with Mr Moar and found him extremely agreeable and obliging. They had white shirts at three different prices, vis four shillings, four and sixpence and seven shillings. I did not think the cheap ones half good enough, so I took one of the best. They are all made without collars now as the loose ones are thought to be the best fitting as well as the handiest. They had no neckties at all that I liked but Mr Moar very kindly went and got a sight of some so I got one which I think will do very nicely. They had seven rolls of flannel but all of them were tartan. They had plenty of ready made flannel shirts, so I took one which Mr Moar recommended as being a very rare and genteel colour.

I have got the cloak and the merino. The cloak is a very pretty one but not very expensive. There were eight yards of merino in the piece and they all assured me that six was too little for a dress in the present style and advised me to take the piece as it was and then if it should leave any it would be good to have suppose I was requiring to alter the dress. I was afraid to take it for thought it would be too much for you to have to pay for, but after considering the matter in every light decided on keeping it.

Aunty has made me a present of a nice dark dress so you will not require to buy me one for the winter and will better afford to pay for the merino. My friends have fairly overwhelmed me with kindness. Uncle Peter says that if he could have got a loan of a gig he would have put us to the Bridge of Walls free of expense. Is not that kind? Oh they have all been so kind.

I was really very much in need of a common dress and yet it was not in my power to procure one and what do you think? When I came to town Aunty had material for one lying waiting me. And besides she has given me a very pretty tablecloth and a veil. She says I must wear a veil and Mrs Tulloch has given me half a dozen towels and a counterpane, half a dozen linen pocket handkerchiefs and six yards of good cotton. And Mrs Malcolmson has given me a crystal butter dish, two jelly dishes and half a dozen tea spoons and Kathy Tait a crystal sugar dish and cream jug. They have all astonished me. I loved them all and I know they liked me but I really did not think they cared quite so much about me.

I would have written more but we happen to be out of paper.

With fondest love,

Your loving little wife,

Barbara

Sandness 16ᵗʰ June 1861

I have not been at church today, darling love. It is either a feast or a famine with us. We had three ministers last sabbath and this one we have none. I rose this morning with the intention of writing you a long letter but I believe I am very selfish and am sorry for it. After breakfast I took up the January number of the "Sunday at Home".

"Notes from an Arctic Diary" by a moravian missionary caught my eye. I read one paper, then another, became intensely interested and could not leave till I had finished and the entire day has been spent in doing it. It is true I have been thinking of you between hands, have said often I must give it up and write, but nothing would arrest my attention but some tremendous iceberg which threatened destruction to the noble ship "Investigator" and I was compelled to proceed.

June is passing away swiftly. We have been busy all week rubbing off the voar rust and the summer evenings do not seem near so long as they did some time ago. A good deal yet remains to be done.

You do not say about what time you expect to be ready. I should like all over and you safely at Sandness while the fine weather lasts. Your father would like Mr Saunders to be at home and it would be much more convenient than to bring a minister from another parish. He has been I suppose at the General Assembly. You are perhaps not aware that in reply to my 'speering' epistle your father said "I may add before closing that we wish as little display as possible and as our house is not fit for a large or brilliant company that there may be as few as possible. I had thought of some, but being unwilling to give offence I have resolved on having none but what is absolutely necessary. We have not beds to keep people over the night and therefore any friends you would have wished you would better have them at home afterwards." I thought this premature as I had never consulted him, but saw at once that my wisest course would be to give up all idea of even proposing any person to be invited and thought no more about it.

"A large or brilliant company" was entirely beyond our means and therefore out of the question. As every friend of mine is excluded I had no idea that I would be expected to stand the expenses of our wedding, but as the company is to be very small and very select, one and all teetotallers, the expense will not surely be a great deal.

Your father explains why your application to the needle has been so incessant. I can appreciate your motives, but am really vexed. I would much rather that you had run an account – all you have earned cannot be much. It has been very thoughtless in me, I ought to have considered. You need have had no hesitation in telling me and I would have sent you the money. Such incessant application is a slavery and I know it is injurious. I am glad to hear that you have now nearly finished and do hope that your labours at the needle morning noon and night are at an end for ever.

This is far from a good letter, but you must give me all your news in return, and after we are married I shall write you splendid love letters and copy them all in a book.

With fondest love, your own devoted

Robert Jamieson

Sandness 24th June 1861

My dearest dearest love

I owe you an apology dearest for not writing you last week. I delayed till Thursday night and as that night chanced to be an unusually busy one I did not have leisure. Often on post nights I have very little time. The people have learned that I can write a little, and four or five of them will come at a time entreating to write either their husbands, their brothers or their sweethearts for them and I find it so difficult to refuse. In time to come I shall be as punctual as a clock and to make sure of it shall write you on either Tuesday or Wednesday evening.

Today I was pleasantly surprised to receive a letter from Mr Tawse stating that an addition of £2 has been made to the school at Sandness – thus raising my salary to £20 per annum. As Sandness is about the best school on the society's scheme in Zetland, very likely some of the other teachers have received more and I shall be glad to hear that your father has received £3 additional. I need not tell you that I am truly well pleased as my income will now amount to £28 per annum exclusive of the farm and I intend to abandon grumbling for ever. The weddings here are far from being over yet. The proclamation fees have this season exceeded my school fees.

Mr C. H. Jamieson is resolved to start a newspaper in Lerwick. I have received the prospectus today. I shall be glad that he succeed, but except on a rare and pressing occasion it is not likely I will contribute much. There is in fact so little here to write about.

My principal servant has been corresponding with a young man for some years and they were to be married in winter. His father has by this post received intelligence of his death. I am very sorry and do not know how I shall tell her. She will very likely be frantic. I feel for her very much. It was only the evening before last that she was telling me how their courtship commenced, how much she loved him, what a fine fellow he was, how he was to come home when he returned off this voyage, and their wedding was an endless theme. To receive such intelligence in the midst of such high expectations is sad indeed. She will very likely go home to her father when she hears it and no persuasion of mine will, I fear, induce her to stay.

Write me by next post, please, tell me how you are progressing.

With fondest love,

Your ever loving, Robert

Gulberwick 13th July 1861

My dear dear Robert

I had been looking forward to the 23rd as our wedding day and am truly sorry to hear that it must be delayed a week longer. I did not know that we had to be proclaimed any more than one Sunday at Sandness and I was not aware that you required any authority from me more than I had given you. I shall be quite ready next week, so you may have us proclaimed when you like. I believe that of the two I am now the most anxious for our marriage. Have I wearied you love? O that I could see you and know that I was forgiven, but once we are married you may punish me any way you like. I shall submit to it cheerfully.

My dress is the best fit I ever had on and the colour becomes me very much. I have got mother's and Eliza's finished too and I have nothing now to do but one or two trifling things. The stairs are up now and the north room is nearly finished.

You want to know who are to be invited. There are none in Gulberwick but Robert Tait's folk, then in Lerwick there is uncle and aunty and Mr and Mrs Tulloch. I had intended Elizabeth Malcolmson for best maid but her mother cannot bear to let her go. If all should come that will be invited there will not be many. I do wish it was over. I am heartily tired of the talking.

I have had a hard struggle between duty and inclination today. There are seven ships of the Channel fleet lying in Lerwick harbour just now and yesterday the band of one of them was ashore playing in the garrison. Maria happened to be in town and she went and heard them and came home quite delighted. Today they are to play again and anybody who chooses may come on board and see the vessels. Oh, how happy I would have been to go and hear the grand music and see the noble vessels, but stern duty compels me to stay at home.

I shall here subjoin little Arthur's prayer.

"O lode make me a gaed sild, new my hat, give my sin and keep me from evil. Biss my dee panents, badis and sistes. Biss my bab and my bob. Chist's sake amen."

You will never have to marry again, I hope, and I'm sure the Sandness folk will not object to your taking a fortnight to yourself at this time. If you could manage to be here say about Wednesday I think that would do very well. Then we could be married the Tuesday following, start for home on Thursday and we could surely be able to reach it by Friday night. So you would not be away a whole fortnight. Please let me hear from you by Friday's post and tell me that you will agree to this plan like a dear good fellow.

With fondest love,

your loving little wife,

Barbara

Sandness 14th July 1861

My Dearest

To look back, it seems but a brief space since I wrote you my first letter and yet it is three and a half years. Our courtship has therefore been rather a long one. There may have been occasionally a very little misunderstanding between us but on the whole a more amiable correspondence was never carried on. You have been faithful and true and I have loved you deeply.

In the future our happiness will depend on a great measure on our selves and if in the evening of our days we can look back on our married life with as much satisfaction as we can do on our days of courtship we will be happy indeed.

The expression "loving little wife" pleased me exceedingly and I wish you had continued to use it, it looked so pretty.

I think you will give up using my surname and address me by my first name, it will be more familiar. And try to learn to say "du" instead of "you".

Your ever true and devoted

Robert

Gulberwick 16th July 1861

My dear dear Robert

I am going to try and learn to use your first name since you wish it though it does not come quite natural to me, but I will not promise to learn to say "du".

You see, when I first became acquainted with you, you were in my estimation rather an elderly person and I have never yet quite got rid of that idea. Then your education was infinitely superior to mine and you had too a more than ordinary share of natural sense. Now all these things made me look up to you which I still do and hope ever will, so I can't say "du" to you. We can be familiar and kindly enough without that.

I am a believer in the old saying "too much familiarity breeds contempt" and I believe it necessary for comfort and happiness that people maintain a proper degree of respect for each other.

Your loving little wife,

Barbara

Robert Jamieson and Barbara Laing were married at

the schoolhouse in Gulberwick on 6th August 1861.

They had six sons and two daughters.

Descriptions of photographs
(all images taken in Shetland)

1858

9.   View from St. Ninians Isle
11. Scord, Scatness
13. Weisdale Voe
15. Ocraquoy, Fladdabister
17. Dale of Walls
19. Sands of Sound
21. Gletness, Nesting
23. Melby, Sandness
25. Gulberwick Beach
27. North Punds, Levenwick
29. Meal Beach, Burra
31. North Punds, Levenwick

1859

33. Ness of Trebister
35. Voxter, South Cunningsburgh
37. Gletness, Nesting
39. Scalloway Castle
41. Funzie, Fetlar
43. Silwick, Wester Skeld
45. Funzie, Fetlar
47. Greenland, Walls
49. Reawick
51. Lerwick

1860

53. Kergord
55. Dale of Walls
57. Brough, Nesting
59. Melby House, Sandness
61. Sandwick
63. Hermaness, Unst
65. Mangaster Voe
67. Bay of Funzie, Fetlar
69. Norby, Sandness
71. St Ninians Isle
73. Trondra
75. Melby, Sandness
77. Sandy Loch, Upper Sound

1861

79.   Hangcliff Lane, Lerwick
81.   Kergord
83.   Gulberwick Kirk
85.   Croft house Museum, Dunrossness
87.   Little Ayre, Muckle Roe
89.   Fethaland
91.   Lerwick
93.   Easter Quarff
95.   Norby, Sandness
97.   St Ninians Isle
99.   Meal Beach, Burra
101. North Punds, Levenwick
103. Silwick, Wester Skeld
105. Huxter, Sandness

Shetland – A Love Story

Postscript

ROBERT and Barbara's daughter, Christina, spent the last years of her life in New Zealand. In poor health, she wrote to her niece, my aunt Barbara, in 1937.

"… I found, just before I left Shetland, that a box in the cock-loft that I had thought held only wool had, under the wool, the mater and pater's love letters. There was not time to sort or burn them, so I bundled them into a tin box, padlocked it and got Mrs Nicolson to take charge of it till I came back. I told her that if I did not return you would look after them.

You will have to take them out to Snarraness and burn them there. Letters do not burn thoroughly if folded or in envelopes and I opened up and crumpled the thousands I burned before I left.

There are probably some you will want to keep. You may find it remarkable that a young woman of nineteen would be attracted to a man eleven years her senior, lame from polio and who walked with two sticks, but I knew the pater and it was never surprising to me.

That box is now preying on my mind …"

I don't know who retrieved the letters, or when, but in 1949 my aunt who was living in Dublin sent them in a chest of drawers, along with other family pieces, to my father in Leeds. The furniture was stored for a while in a warehouse in Huddersfield where there was a fire. Our furniture survived and the letters eventually passed to me.

About 40 years ago I began to read them, but when I found one from Robert saying, "I have a secret drawer for your letters so that the eye of no living being will ever see them but my own. I shall treasure them like gems", I felt like an intruder and put them to one side.

Ten years ago my cousin Norna (a grand-daughter of Robert and Barbara) who had retired to Reawick told me she thought they would make interesting reading and when I quoted that extract she looked at me with exaggerated patience and said, "Oh, I think 150 years is a decent enough interval".

KW

Sandness
30th July 1860

I cannot be mistaken - You are
worthy of being loved -

The reason why I did
not come East at the time I mentioned was,
after I wro
intimation
... of Reg
... here a
He came
here if my
house was
... week
the arrival
... from
that by this time your house
will be nearly furnished. and
will prove fully more comfortable
and will look amaist as well

However anxious I might
... thing to
... writing
... for a ...
... respect
... I think
... a speed
it was
it ought
much
... on
... sor
... we ye
And never will - You still oc
casionally glide past - I see you
look - I hear you laugh - I listen
for a moment to an enchanting

Mr Robert Jamieson
Schoolmaster
Sandness